"Ronne Rock is the real deal, and so are the people she's featured in this book. The stories inside will serve as an encouragement to dare beyond what you thought was possible. Get ready for a new look at the influence you have in your world and your neighborhood."

Jon Acuff, *New York Times* bestselling author

"I love storytelling and I love brave women. And by brave, I mean those who say yes to God and renounce what they've built with their own strength. Ronne shares very detailed and beautiful accounts of some powerful relationships God has provided to shape her life and strengthen her walk of faith. As president of the Latin American Christian Alliance for Orphans, I especially treasured reading the sincere narrative about that encounter with her own limitations in her former approach to caring for the vulnerable. Our default mode is to barge in and try quick fixes instead of humbly asking more questions and coming alongside those who are already doing the hard, beautiful work of obeying God in ways the world may regard as "slow" or less impactful.

May this book inspire you to see Jesus as that pearl of great price and to say yes to whatever it is He's calling you to so that you can fulfill your purpose, which is to glorify His wondrous Name through the work of justice he has prepared beforehand."

Aixa de López, international speaker, president of Latin America Christian Alliance for Orphans, and author of *Lágrimas Valientes*

"Loving and serving others is not a ⟨...⟩ duty as Christians. Many want to ⟨...⟩ few actually pack their bags and ⟨...⟩ well and change lives. Ronne Rock i⟨...⟩ who makes a profound differenc⟨...⟩ she's willing to go. An incredible word weaver who engages the reader with raw truth, Ronne's stories will thoroughly draw you

in, making you feel like the women whose tales she tells are right in your living room. She shares real conversations with women who are living messy and broken but truth-filled lives and are willing to share the good, bad, and ugly bits of life. She shows miraculous grace in the midst of devastating circumstances, reminding women that our God is the God of the ampersand, the God of also/and, not either/or. She proves that each of us can change the world if we're willing to simply go."

Kate Battistelli, speaker, mentor, and author
of *The God Dare* and *Growing Great Kids*

"*One Woman Can Change the World* is filled to the brim with stories of everyday women displaying heroic faith in difficult situations. Come and learn what it means to be a hope-filled woman in your context through the beauty of these Christian women from around the world. Inspiring!"

Mary DeMuth, author of forty books,
including *Outrageous Grace Every Day*

"Ronne Rock's heart beats for women to see their God-given potential realized. She gives her whole heart in pursuit of this endeavor, but in the process she has learned that the greatest teachers are sometimes the very people we're trying to serve. In this collection of stories, we see strength, resilience, hope, leadership, and dignity on display through women around the world who we'd otherwise never have the opportunity to meet. *One Woman Can Change the World* is a story of becoming in which we all might see ourselves—and our design—a little more clearly."

Adriel Booker, speaker, advocate, and author
of *Grace Like Scarlett*

"I'm writing these words tearful, agog, and thankful. How does Ronne Rock know so much about me—as a woman, a daughter of God, as someone working in the world to make some small difference? Through her empathetic voice and brilliant stories from her own life and the lives of unlikely heroines from around the world, I feel known, heard, seen, and better equipped to keep loving my small world into a better place. Five stars!"

Leslie Leyland Fields, author of *Your Story Matters*

"For any woman asking where her gifts fit into her local community or whether she has anything of value to offer the world, this book is both a guide and mentor. Ronne artistically weaves the stories of women around the world, whose lives are so different from ours, into a communal tapestry of strength, dignity, purpose, and destiny. A tapestry that acts like a treasure map, revealing who we are and what our God-given purpose is. This book left me empowered and ready to take action, confident that I'm part of a global community of strong, grace-filled women whose God is for them and with them."

Niki Hardy, author of *Breathe Again*

"Ronne Rock has witnessed strong, humble women quietly, faithfully serving God around the world, and their examples have transformed the way she views her purpose and potential as a Christian leader. In *One Woman Can Change the World*, Ronne's vulnerable testimony—combined with the testimonies of the women—invites us to view with fresh eyes our own potential to lead and serve others."

Ann Kroeker, writing coach, author of *Not So Fast*, and coauthor of *On Being a Writer*

"We gals are world changers. But we often prevent ourselves from living as one. In *One Woman Can Change the World*, Ronne Rock captures the essence of this struggle, helping women reclaim their God-given voice, strength, and purpose. This book is a much-needed, contemporary kaleidoscope of inspiring stories. It's for every not-so-little-girl who believes she shouldn't or couldn't change the world for the better."

Tracy Steel, speaker and author of *A Redesigned Life*

ONE
WOMAN
CAN
CHANGE
THE
WORLD

ONE WOMAN CAN CHANGE THE WORLD

RECLAIMING YOUR GOD-DESIGNED INFLUENCE
AND IMPACT RIGHT WHERE YOU ARE

Ronne Rock

Revell

a division of Baker Publishing Group
Grand Rapids, Michigan

© 2020 by Ronne Rock

Published by Revell
a division of Baker Publishing Group
PO Box 6287, Grand Rapids, MI 49516-6287
www.revellbooks.com

Printed in the United States of America

Library of Congress Cataloging-in-Publication Data
Names: Rock, Ronne, 1959- author.
Title: One woman can change the world : reclaiming your God-designed influence and impact right where you are / Ronne Rock.
Description: Grand Rapids, Michigan : Revell, a division of Baker Publishing Group, 2020. | Includes bibliographical references.
Identifiers: LCCN 2019055675 | ISBN 9780800736989
Subjects: LCSH: Leadership—Religious aspects. | Leadership in women. | Christian women—Religious life.
Classification: LCC BL65.L42 R63 2020 | DDC 204/.4082—dc23
LC record available at https://lccn.loc.gov/2019055675

Unless otherwise indicated, Scripture quotations are from THE MESSAGE, copyright © 1993, 1994, 1995, 1996, 2000, 2001, 2002 by Eugene H. Peterson. Used by permission of NavPress. All rights reserved. Represented by Tyndale House Publishers, Inc.

Scripture quotations labeled CEB are from the COMMON ENGLISH BIBLE. © Copyright 2011 COMMON ENGLISH BIBLE. All rights reserved. Used by permission. (www.CommonEnglishBible.com).

Scripture quotations labeled CEV are from the Contemporary English Version © 1991, 1992, 1995 by American Bible Society. Used by permission.

Scripture quotations labeled NLT are from the *Holy Bible*, New Living Translation, copyright © 1996, 2004, 2007, 2013, 2015 by Tyndale House Foundation. Used by permission of Tyndale House Publishers, Inc., Carol Stream, Illinois 60188. All rights reserved.

Scripture quotations labeled NLV are from the New Life Version. Copyright © 1969, 2003 by Barbour Publishing, Inc.

Scripture quotations labeled TPT are from The Passion Translation®. Copyright © 2017 by BroadStreet Publishing® Group, LLC. Used by permission. All rights reserved.

Scripture quotations labeled VOICE are from the Voice Bible. Copyright © 2012 Thomas Nelson, Inc. The Voice™ translation © 2012 Ecclesia Bible Society. All rights reserved.

The author is represented by the literary agency of Credo Communications, LLC, Grand Rapids, Michigan, www.credocommunications.net.

Some names and details have been changed to protect the privacy of the individuals involved.

20 21 22 23 24 25 26   7 6 5 4 3 2

Hi there, Miss Mary. I still hear your voice asking,
"Where's your book, love? People need to hear our story."
I can't wait to give this to you.
Here's our book. Here's our story.
Thank you for believing.

I will offer You my grateful heart, for I am Your unique creation, filled with wonder and awe. You have approached even the smallest details with excellence; Your works are wonderful; I carry this knowledge deep within my soul.

Psalm 139:14 VOICE

Contents

Prologue

I cannot but
Love,
Because
My job is "to love"
And I am busy
Loving . . .

Mind you,
It is the most difficult job
Because
Loving is to be "Christ-like"

Because
Our Love is not
"because of" kind of Love,
Instead, it is
Love "in spite of" . . .

May the God of Love
Continue to bless and guide us.

Lucy, founder of Gan Sabra
HIV Home, Aizawl, India

I plopped myself down at the hotel lobby bar and ordered a charcuterie board and a drink from Olivia, the employee working behind the counter. It had been a full day, and my computer waited upstairs—ready for me to do a little more work and a lot of writing. I had three glorious hours to get things done.

A gentleman sat down next to me and ordered a drink as well. "I'm meeting a friend who's staying here," he said as he introduced himself. He had just moved back to Texas after a long haul in a state up north. We chatted about work and faith and family. He told me about his daughter, who worked for a church and loved to serve in Nicaragua. Then he told me about his son, who died by suicide. I told him about organizations like To Write Love on Her Arms and guys like Carlos Whittaker who are helping to tell a better story about mental health. The man wept.

Through his tears, he told me about a special water garden in town that his son had loved. He couldn't wait to visit it again. We talked about heaven and how close it really is. He said he was ready to spend time with his daughter, because she was the strong one. His friend called to tell him he was at the wrong hotel, so he said his good-byes, but not before giving me a polite hug and a thank-you. I told him he was the one to be thanked. The conversation had eternity wrapped up in it.

All the while, Olivia worked. She and a shuttle driver were the only staff present to serve a packed hotel. As the front desk clerk, Olivia did it all—checked in guests, served food and drinks, answered phone calls, made sure laundry was delivered, called for cars, calmed frustrations, and did her best to learn a brand-new snack menu. And she smiled the entire time. "That woman is a fireball," the man had said as he prepared to leave. "She hasn't slowed down. She'll own this place someday."

Olivia is also in school. As she worked, she shared with me that she hopes to be in management someday so she can take care of employees the way she wants to take care of customers. She knows what it feels like to be overlooked, so she does everything she can to make sure every guest feels welcomed. "I fail sometimes," she said, "but I keep at it."

I'd gone to the lobby bar for a quick meal so I could get back to the evening I had so carefully planned. I ended up being disrupted by Jesus. He was there in the dreams of a young woman, and He was there in the grief of a dad who was eager to see the daughter he wished he was more like. I'm praying for both of them even now. And I'm hoping the hotel gives Olivia a promotion.

As I walked to the elevator, I heard Olivia take a request for a wake-up call. "Yes, ma'am. That's three thirty. In the a.m.? You've got it! Sweet dreams, ma'am!"

I want to be more like Olivia. She wants to change the world, one customer at a time. I think we all do, really. Whether we work at a hotel or own our own chain of them, conduct meetings in high-powered boardrooms or gather kids around the kitchen table to talk about chores, you and I were born with eyes to see the potential for better days. It's built into the way we actually perceive the things around us, built into the gut feelings we have and the way we somehow gather strength in the midst of the darkest trials. Olivia reminded me of the persistence we women have deep within us to believe restoration is a reality.

For Olivia, that restoration is customer service and employee satisfaction. For you, that restoration may be the safety of a neighborhood or kindness shown to strangers—or rebuilding the love that's been shattered within your own family. You and I have big dreams. We have things that prick at us like cactus needles, things that get our attention and hold it and insist that we do something. Born in the image and likeness of God, we are creators at heart.

I believe we as women are leaders at heart too. And I believe one woman can change the world, because I've seen it.

Some of you are nodding your heads right now. I'm warning you in advance that this book may mess with you.

Many of you are saying, "Wait a second—I may be able to lead a bit, but I'm no *leader*. And change the world? You've got the wrong woman."

I don't. I promise.

I write articles to help leaders do their jobs better, and there's a lot of "Five Powerful Ways" and "Three Tips" language in them. Tips and tricks are great for things like interviews, debriefs, and how to encourage your staff and volunteer teams. But tips and tricks fall short when it comes to the way we live our lives.

This may be a book filled with leaders, but it's not a typical leadership book. This book isn't a prescription, and it's not filled with bulleted next steps for getting the perfect promotion or finally cracking the code to starting your own empire. Nor does this book offer up perfect models for business or ministry. What the women in these pages have to share is far more beautiful than these things. *This is a book about who you and I are as women.*

You may not always agree with the decisions each woman featured has made on her journey. You may not always agree with me either. That's okay.

Consider this book more of a conversation between you and me about things we've been told, things we've come to believe, and things we fear simply because we're human—since being human can be viewed as a pretty big flaw, *unless* you see humanity as divinely designed. Think of this book as a peek into the very real lives of very real women. Each of them has fought fear. Each of them has at times questioned herself or worried she'd be found lacking in a world that loves to define us by what we do rather than who we are. These women battle self-loathing, mental illness, loneliness. They battle their pasts. They battle oppression and bias and scorn. There are days when all goes well and days when knees are bloodied from stumbling. And yet they still believe they are designed by God to make an impact and influence the world.

They're teaching me to believe that too.

Oh, and this book doesn't really end—because these women's lives aren't over.

Our lives aren't over either.

Think of this book as a note of encouragement, a reminder that everything about you—the good days, the hard seasons, the feelings you feel and the way you think, the person who looks back at you when you look in the mirror, and the person who shows up to overwhelm your thoughts when you take the time to listen— yes, *everything* about you is purposeful and meaningful and has a place in your story.

This is an honest look at what it means to be a woman of influence in a world that often doesn't make leadership easy. It's about leading with grace in cultures that aren't always graceful. It's about reclaiming all your God-given physical and spiritual DNA and allowing it to do its work in and through you.

I'm a marketer, a storyteller, a lover of #kitchentherapy, a walk-the-long-road kind of gal who doesn't weary easily when the stories get messy. The stories in this book are just that. They're observations gathered from living life with other women here in the United States and around the world, and they're observations gathered from my "Jesus and coffee" times in the mornings.

But they're also far more than observations. They are a part of my own long-road journey of transformation; these women who are changing the world have changed my own in the process. As I've put pen to paper (or fingers to keyboard), I've relived every single one of the struggles in these chapters—and I've been reminded over and over again that the Lord is ever faithful and ever present.

This book is unapologetically written through the lens of faith. Though the women in this book differ in terms of culture, background, and beliefs, the one thing that holds us all together is Christ's love for us. It's that love that compels us all.

This book is an adventure of sorts. It will take you to places like the majestic Himalayas and lush Jamaican hillside villages—and

Grand Rapids, Michigan (which is also beautiful, by the way). I want these stories to inspire you to embrace the abundance of all that God has poured into you and, more than anything, to fall in love with people and their stories.

And this book is a promise made good to Miss Mary. You'll get to know her as you read. Everyone who meets her can't help but fall in love with her after receiving her encouragement as well as what might be one of the best and biggest and longest hugs in the Caribbean.

You see, it was Miss Mary who asked what I was doing with what I had been given. It was her tenacious hope that followed me home from a visit to the tiny community of Eden, Jamaica, where she served at the Jamaican Christian School for the Deaf.

I remember the day she tapped me on the shoulder as I sat on the front stoop of the school's dining hall. With gentleness she said, "You need to tell our story. What are you waiting for, love?" It was her story and her prompting that opened my eyes to see the stories all around me—stories of women willing to believe that restoration can be a reality on earth as it is in heaven.

Yes, it was Miss Mary who came to mind first when I thought of what my friend Tom said about women.

I stepped off the bus in Kenya and onto a rutted orange clay road that would lead our mission team to the Madeleine School, a safe haven for children and their families in a rural farming village near the Ugandan border. I breathed in the familiar developing-country smell of burning fields and listened to a song in the distance, the haunting trill of voices celebrating our arrival.

Though it was the weekend, children stood in uniforms along the road, clapping and looking for the faces of their sponsors. A few men welcomed us, all teachers at the school. But the celebration was found in the women. They danced and sang, taking hold of our hands and raising them to the sky in the most glorious of celebrations as we moved like a river to the school, where we would be adorned with leis and honored like royalty. The women never stopped singing and lifting their voices in jubilant cries of praise that began in the depths of their souls and crashed joyously into the heavens.

I looked at Tom, the Orphan Outreach in-country leader, with tears in my eyes. "Oh, this is divine. But where are all the men? Are they at work?"

He responded with a smile. "In our country, when it comes to the important things—the things that count—women take the lead."

Women like Miss Mary. Women like Olivia. Women like you and me.

Introduction

We Have No Milk

First thing in the morning, she dresses for work,
    rolls up her sleeves, eager to get started.
She senses the worth of her work,
    is in no hurry to call it quits for the day.

Proverbs 31:17–18

Does anyone truly know where a story begins? Does a journey start with a first step, or does it begin much earlier—when those steps are being contemplated? Or even earlier, when the sojourner is on a completely different journey and blissfully unaware of the ruts and twists in the tilt-a-whirl road she can't yet see?

This journey, my journey, could begin in any number of places and points in time. I have decorated entire walls with sticky notes to decipher which beginning is the most attractive and marketable and then sat silently, remembering what I've been taught by the women who don't fuss much about which story is going to get the most attention.

21

The women have changed me. I am still being changed.

Chances are you've not met these women before, unless you've been blessed to have stumbled upon their work. I can't wait to introduce them to you. Did you know that I actually set out to write a story about each of them with a goal of raising money to help build a school or two? Yeah, I thought I had it all figured out. I had a great plan of building a charity case that would woo you and win you over. That's what I do for a living—craft clever content all tied up with shiny, call-to-action bows.

But I'm getting ahead of myself, because this story, the story of how the women have changed me, began years before my great idea. In fact, it began long before I realized I was being changed.

It was September 2009, and I was standing next to my best friend, Courtney, in a place that looked like something out of a Tolkien novel, captivated by the world around me.

Perfect Plans, Polished Words

On the outskirts of Quetzaltenango, Guatemala, cinder-block buildings seemed to tumble down a hill surrounded by stark cliffs and yellow flowers that bloomed in crevices. The air reminded me of springtime rain showers in Texas. The afternoon sky darkened, and soon the clouds danced at our feet.

"I've never seen anything like this before," Courtney said as we moved through the mist and listened to the sound of laughter coming from the building behind us. It wasn't our first short-term mission trip, but it was my first time leading a team. I had attended a two-day training session and had received high praise from the instructors. My backpack was filled with money, insurance papers, itineraries, and emergency numbers, along with a notebook containing every detail of what the coming days would bring. Courtney's backpack had everything needed for painting and crafts.

I wanted to do ministry, but I wanted even more to do something significant. I had created a blog to share the all-important stories and had promised to send compelling words to the mission-sending agency too.

The night before, I had written my first post in anticipation of a day at the children's home. After worshiping at a church in Guatemala City, we had boarded a bus to traverse the winding roads pocked and pitted by mudslides.

"We ventured carefully up the narrow cobblestone streets leading to our hotel, a few of us reflecting on our time spent in this city a year ago when we traveled to deliver shoes to government homes. This trip was going to be far different than simply distributing shoes, as we prepared for ministry to an orphanage with seventy-two children, all removed from abusive circumstances. We painted T-shirts and wrote memory verses on index cards. And we were reminded to fear not. To love wholly. To allow our hearts to be wrecked by those sweet faces." The words on my blog were as spit polished and well placed as the plans in my backpack.

Children ranging in age from two to sixteen were at the orphanage, all cared for by Lourdes and Teresa, two sisters who'd chosen to follow their parents from Mexico. Years before our trip, their father had grand dreams of ministering to families, but when he saw abuse and neglect raging around him, he knew he had to do something. He prayed and decided to make a safe home for kids. His homeland questioned the move to another country that wouldn't welcome him easily. His new country questioned his sincerity and worth.

People mocked him when he purchased the land that tilted dangerously toward a rushing river. With stern dedication, the family worked to build a home for the little ones who desperately needed a place to stay. He welcomed the children into Pequeño Refugio, "Little House of Refuge." He saw it as a place of healing. He mapped out his plans to restore the crumbling, cobweb-filled buildings on the property and perhaps even build a home for his own family. He, his wife, and his daughters set to work on his dream.

But then he died.

The two sisters, one a former doctor and one a former teacher, stepped into their dad's shoes. Though secretly they wondered if they could truly follow in his footsteps, they never hesitated to continue his legacy, never dreamed of returning to Mexico and their careers and thoughts of marriage and starting their own families. Two other women joined them to help prepare meals, teach, counsel, and keep enemies at bay. More women were added as they cared for a growing number of children who were rescued from abuse and neglect. And then, without knowing much about us, they welcomed our team onto the hillside with the crumbling cinder block and yellow flowers. And we gladly came, laden with good intentions and duffel bags full of stuff.

We had lice shampoo, Neosporin, a random assortment of school supplies, and loads of pipe cleaners. I'm not sure what the pipe cleaners were for, but we had been told that everything in the duffel bags was essential at orphanages. We piled the duffels in the corner of a makeshift library where some girls were doing homework, introduced ourselves, and then promptly grabbed our paintbrushes to work on a room used for quiet time and study.

A few hours later, we abandoned the painting project to spend time with the kids. Rain began to fall as we passed out bandanas and organized teams, then launched into a competition to see which team would be first to memorize a Scripture passage about overcoming fear. To our surprise, there was no competition at all. The children recited the passage quickly, as if they already knew it. Courtney then distributed T-shirts for the kids to decorate, while I worked diligently to keep us on track as the downpour threatened our perfectly scripted day.

I Think We've Got This Backwards

"Honestly, this is amazing," I remarked to a team member who beamed as the kids recited their memory verse another time. "The kids are really connecting with us—our team is doing so well."

I smiled and glanced over at the sisters, who watched as the mission team danced and played with the children, expecting them to be delighted with what they saw.

Instead, the sisters stood to the side, cautiously observing all that was happening around them as if suspicious of our presence. I wanted so much to know what was going on inside their heads. I wanted to help them—really help them. Though I had worked in the nonprofit world for only a short while, I was a go-getter with years of experience in making things happen. My head was filled with statistics on orphan care, and I was a wizard at coming up with great ideas. This was the first time a mission team like ours had visited Pequeño Refugio, and I wanted more than anything to make an impact. I really wanted the children and the sisters to love us. And I wanted everyone in America to love them.

We wrapped up our first-day plans and gave each of the kids a piece of candy. The older sister looked concerned. "Please, only one piece for each child. We do not feed them much sugar."

Warm fragrances from the kitchen filled the hallway, and we said our farewells to four older girls who were assigned dining room duty for the evening meal. As the team walked to the bus, I casually turned and walked down the hallway to the sisters, who were standing with the children. "This was a great day, right? We'll see you tomorrow. You want us to finish painting, yes? You know we're going into town for the night, and we're more than happy to bring back anything you might need."

To this day, I have no idea what I thought they might say. I was raised to always ask if folks needed anything—and with all the kids, perhaps they were running low on toilet paper or peanut butter.

The sisters looked at each other, and then Lourdes calmly said, "We have no milk."

I stood there, unable to find any worthy words. As a translator asked more questions, I learned they hadn't had milk for weeks, and they hadn't had any meat for months.

Quietly, I turned and walked toward the bus, where Courtney and the rest of the Americans were waiting. "Okay, guys, so here's the deal. This place—it has no milk for the kids," I shared as my voice cracked under the weight of reality. Courtney sighed. "This kills me. We brought pipe cleaners, and they have no milk."

Frustration, anger, and heartbreak filled the space around us. "Why in the world did we bring school supplies?" asked one team member as I looked down at the notebook that was filled with great plans and good intentions to help that were proving not to be very helpful at all. From the back of the bus, we heard, "I've got some cash. Can we go to the store?"

The words were like breath, and the team quickly rallied. We pulled together more than four hundred dollars in a few minutes, drove to the city center, and purchased dry milk, Incaparina (a vitamin-fortified beverage that our translators told us was excellent for little ones who struggled with solid food), and meat.

Back at the hotel that night, the atmosphere was weighty. There were no high fives or eloquent stories shared. There were only questions with few answers. In tears, Courtney looked at the Bible lesson we were planning to teach the next day. "*Fear not*. Wow. Right. Here we are thinking *we* are going to come in and teach *them* about trusting God. I think we've got this backwards."

I posted an update to the blog filled with flowery language about the wonderful work that had been done and the tender affection of the children toward us. There was no mention of the conversation in the hallway or the gathering of the money or the shattering of pride—my pride.

I went to bed in tears. I was heartbroken, embarrassed, and ashamed that we could come with such gloriously misguided intent. But then anger set in as I stared at the ceiling and walked back through every moment of the day. *What kind of place is this anyway?* I seethed. *Why did we bring all this crap with us if it's not what's really needed? How could these women let their orphanage run out of milk, for goodness' sake? If kids are starving, why aren't they doing something about it? AND WHY ARE THEY SO CALM?*

Lourdes and Teresa had not begged. There had been no tears or heartfelt pleas. Had I not asked, they wouldn't have mentioned anything. There was simply a "We have no milk," spoken in the same tone as you or I might use to say, "We're running low on detergent."

I tried to understand these women who had walked away from successful careers to follow their calling. Only two years earlier, I had done the same. I had left a very comfortable six-figure life to join the nonprofit world, taking all my marketing prowess and worldly wisdom with me.

I had been taught to believe that any problem could be solved with a few clarifying questions and a three-step plan. Today's problem was milk. *Milk.*

I wanted so badly to fix the problem. I wanted to rush back to the United States and climb on my soapbox and loudly expose the injustice. To launch a clever campaign to make sure there would *never* not be milk—because I knew how to do things. I wanted to teach these women how to get things done. Why did I feel so helpless to help them?

True Leadership

The next morning we returned to the orphanage. The children greeted us on the dirt drive, dancing when they saw the groceries. "Leche! Leche!" they exclaimed as they grabbed the bags of powdered milk and ran to the kitchen. Courtney prayed with our team as I talked to the sisters. "We're ready to paint—got our work clothes on and everything. Where do you want us to start?"

Teresa smiled and said, "We think you would like to see our home this morning. Would you let us do that first?"

The time for painting would come, but right now it was clear: the sisters had something to say.

And so we walked. And we listened.

And the sisters who seemed too meek, too quiet to be in charge of anything taught us all about true leadership.

We Want This to Be a Home

We walked up stairs overlooking a field that served as both a back-yard for the children and a grazing area for two old goats. My heart caught in my throat when I saw the second-floor landing. It was like artwork, a patchwork mosaic of marble and stone in rich burnished colors. "Oh, this is exquisite!" I exclaimed. "Who designed it?"

"We did," Lourdes said. "We have not a lot of money, so we must find ways to make this a home. We traveled to the city and went from contractor to contractor, asking for whatever scraps they had. We knew they couldn't sell broken tiles, so we offered to take them—that way they wouldn't have to throw them away. There is always a way, you see. The Lord always makes a way."

They then walked us into a group of rooms where the younger girls slept. There was a cozy living area with a sofa and a rocker, and the bunk beds were adorned with floral bedspreads and stuffed animals. Next to each bed was a small closet with ruffled curtains.

Again, the sisters shared stories of gathering up fabric remnants to make sure every girl had a special place to call her own. "Would you like to know a secret?" asked Lourdes. She walked over to one of the closets and pulled back the curtain. It was a cardboard box. "Furniture would be nice, but what is important is a personal place for clothes. Today, we use boxes. There is always a way to make a way."

Remnants. Broken tiles. Cardboard. Things I would discard as worthless were given worth in this place. People were given worth here too. There wasn't one paid employee on staff. The two sisters, plus nine workers, offered their time in trade for a place to call home. "We have found that people want a family. Kids. Adults. We want to be family for people. We remember our home. And we want this to be a home."

The tour continued as they showed us the boys' rooms, which were in the middle of a makeover involving remnants of cloth fashioned into bedspreads and pillows. The sisters told us which parts of the building had electricity and the challenges they continually encountered with keeping food safe and dry. The statements were made with the same calm tone as the one that had turned us upside down the day before. Neither sister asked for help. "We know that God will provide. He has always provided. He knows we are here. So we remain here."

We walked by a faded plaque nailed to the side of the building. A donation had been made in the name of Jesus by strangers from the United States. Teresa glanced at the plaque, then quickly turned away and sighed.

We Would Like for It to Last

"You would like to paint now?" Teresa asked.

"Yeah, I think we'd like that," I responded.

Courtney smiled, tears glistening. "Their normal is our anything but, isn't it?" she whispered. "Maybe their normal is better."

We walked into another dorm room where the older girls were gathered on one of the bunk beds, talking about life and school. On another bed, two girls were reading their Bibles. "Yes, they love Scripture," said Lourdes. "They like to memorize it," she said with a gleam in her eye.

Courtney laid out the brushes and poured paint into pans for the team. "How would you like us to decorate the walls?" she asked.

"Well, what if we let the girls tell you what they'd like?" was the response.

One girl smiled and asked, "Maybe we can help too?"

Brushes in hand, the team tucked in behind beds to paint. Hearts and ribbons and flowers were the requests of the girls that day, with a cross and a puppy thrown in for good measure. Small and large hands moved the colors across the walls as conversations about favorite foods and books and Bible stories filled the room.

The sisters were attentive to it all, watching every brushstroke and pointing out where they'd like to see just one more design. "The girls have wanted this for a long time," Lourdes said. "You don't want to just leave a sign on the wall saying you helped. You are the first people to want to do something good—to paint for them. We would like for it to last."

I felt her words shoot through me like an arrow.

The pieces of the days moved into place like the broken tiles that had become mosaics on the floor, revealing such beauty and purpose. I felt my heart shattering and moving into a new place too: the idea that I knew so much, the thought that we were coming to fix and save, the compassion thwarted by pious pity.

I no longer wanted to teach the women anything. Instead, I wished I could roll back time, begin again, and ask them to teach each of us how to stand and walk and rest in a faith that had more heft to it than I had ever felt or seen.

Now they simply wanted to know that a group of people from the United States cared enough to *keep* caring. They didn't want our duffel bags filled with supplies. They didn't care about the bandanas and T-shirts. They wanted to know if we wanted to know about their days—the days that would be lived after we piled onto a bus and drove away.

The painting finished, we gathered the girls and prayed for the house—for safety, for mercy, for it to be a welcoming place. And we prayed to return.

"How may we serve you?" Courtney asked as we cleared away the drop cloths and buckets.

"Yes, we want to serve you. We want to serve the kids," I agreed.

Teresa smiled. "Just spend time with the children today. Play with them. Maybe draw a picture or read a book. We believe time is the best offering."

I Want to Be Like You

I had wanted to give the women my expert advice, my marketing genius, my quick-fix plans to solve problems. And all they asked for was my time. They knew true leadership had to be relational to be transformational. And yet they weren't trying to be leaders. They were simply taking one step and then the next. That was the leadership they lived.

That afternoon the rain began to fall again. In the dining room, I could hear our team singing and clapping. Then the voices changed. It was the voices of the children. They were singing to us. "*Jesús, yo te amo . . .*"

I walked outside to feel the raindrops on my face and the mist beneath my feet. The yellow flowers clinging to the cliffs above me seemed more vivid than before. I shouted, "Esperanza! Oh my gosh—it's esperanza." Flowers of hope that bloomed in my hometown were blooming here too. I breathed in the damp air and ran my hands across the cinder-block walls of the orphanage that only days before had been part of a well-crafted plan to do projects on a mission trip.

A hand on my shoulder brought me back to the afternoon with the children singing in the dining room. It was Teresa. "I want to thank you," she said. "Your time here has been an answer to prayer."

"Yes, I think it has," I stumbled. "This place—you and Lourdes—I want to be like you." As I said the words, I wondered if it was possible. Stepping away from success, walking calmly in scarcity, seeing worth in things deemed worthless. But there was something about the way Lourdes and Teresa led, the way they served, that made me want to try.

PART 1

RECLAIMING YOUR DESIGN

Like an artist in control of His painting, God is sovereign, or in complete control, over all of creation and over my life as well. God uses His own "principle of movement" so that no matter how many figurative bridges I travel across or orange-and-yellow skies I look upon, the eyes of my heart always come back to Him, the focus point of my life. The specific ways God loves, stretches, heals, takes away, or gives are elements of curves, straight lines, and colors that artists use to catch our attention. All of these direct the eyes of our heart back to God as we move from one season of life to another.

from *A Redesigned Life* by Tracy Steel,
speaker and author

So God created human beings in his own image. In the image of God he created them; male and female he created them. . . . Then God looked over all he had made, and he saw that it was very good!

Genesis 1:27, 31 NLT

She's up before dawn, preparing breakfast
for her family and organizing her day.

Proverbs 31:15

1

The Trouble with Women

I was raised to be fierce.

I'm talking about the pull-myself-up-by-my-bootstraps, it-will-be-easier-if-I-just-do-this-myself, I-don't-want-to-be-a-problem mind-set that was born within me and nurtured for the longest time by a mom and a fiery older cousin who wanted to make sure I could take care of myself. I learned to cook at a young age, got my first job at twelve, and was taught to drive a car at thirteen. Both Mom and Julia, whom I named JuJu when I was a toddler, were hell-bent on me being able to get from here to there without ever having to ask for help. My mom said that was what women needed to do in order not to be a burden in this world.

I was raised to believe a lot of things—that sliced bananas and Miracle Whip on white bread make the perfect sandwich, that one dog is a pet but two dogs are just dogs, that wide hips are "breeder's hips" and I should be thankful I was born with them, and that all men just want women for sex and cooking (though her words were far more colorful).

The Bed You Make

Mom met my dad in a bar at the tender age of nineteen and, in a most scandalous move, hopped in a sedan a few weeks later and drove with him from Virginia to Oklahoma City, where they married in his boss's living room. Dad was twelve years Mom's senior, with two failed marriages under his belt and a bottle never far from reach—his means of washing away regret.

A passionate entrepreneur, Dad gave everything he had to the businesses he wanted to build. Those who knew him professionally saw him as a benevolent man with a perpetual smirk and a work ethic like no other. Those who knew him after business hours saw a man tormented by images of World War II and feelings of inadequacy and failure. He decided it was best that Mom not get a driver's license for fear she would simply leave and never return.

Their marriage was a tumultuous one. Dad made threats against both Mom and me whenever he got drunk, and even as a small child I asked Mom why they stayed together if they hated each other so much. She would force a smile and say, "You have to lie in the bed you make."

She had watched her own mother faithfully love her father through ups and downs as they worked together on the farmland he had cultivated in a dot of a town in the Shenandoah Valley. She wanted a marriage like her parents but no part of the small town life, so she proudly bragged to her friends and family that she had been promised a better life with all the trappings. By the time I was born, Mom felt trapped and alone, and she wanted to make sure I didn't follow in her footsteps.

JuJu, on the other hand, was a feisty renegade from childhood. She grew up with a doting Christian mom and hardworking dad, graduated early, and promptly attended business school so she could begin her climb up the corporate ladder. When advancement seemed distant because she didn't have a formal degree, she went back to school to focus on accounting. When the oil and gas company in which she'd invested decades downsized and offered early retirement, she took it—only to then find another job working for the county to ensure her financial security. She traveled the world and considered marriage only two times in her life. Both times she dove in with fierce passion. Both times she was rejected. With determination, JuJu focused her heart on her career, her family, and her own independence. And she was just as determined to make sure I did the same.

My own footsteps fell somewhere in between. I was a high achiever in high school and received scholarships to college for journalism—only to step away from my degree to get married and have a little one.

Years later, thanks to the kindness of a friend who drove all day in her Plymouth Arrow to stand guard as I filled her car with clothes and baby supplies, I fled what had become a thorny situation. I returned to the University of Oklahoma and graduated with a bachelor of arts degree in journalism. I did it while working full-time and caring for my incredible son. My career was fast-tracked, fueled by the providence and favor of a very good heavenly Father, a string of both male and female bosses who believed in and encouraged me, and the work ethic of that alcoholic dad and renegade cousin.

I learned that my mom was right—and wrong. Some men were in fact jerks. But most weren't. I learned that my cousin was right—and wrong. Learning how to change a tire was a smart thing to do. Keeping people at arm's length wasn't.

And yet I was fierce.

Along the way, I met a prince of a man who found joy in all but my love for banana and Miracle Whip sandwiches. We married, he adopted that incredible son of mine, and we all were given wings to explore big dreams. There was Jesus and coffee in the mornings, followed by pushing for success every day. Even when I took the leap from corporate life to the nonprofit world, I still thought every problem could be solved with a brainstorming session and a list of clever action steps.

The True Enemy

When Lourdes and Teresa told me they had no milk or meat, when they showed me closets made from cardboard and floors tiled with scraps, I realized how naive my this-is-all-you-need-to-do mindset was. There was a calm to them that felt disruptive, a creativity within them that was far more vibrant than anything I had experienced in my career, a strength in them that wasn't steeped in pull-yourself-up-and-do-it-on-your-own independence. Neither woman was living the life she had carefully planned or the life her culture said was the norm. But both women were living a life I longed to understand. Instead of brokenness, they saw restoration. Instead of divots and dead ends, they saw the next natural step. Instead of being limited by or angry about gender or pedigree or position, they embraced it all.

I wonder what Lourdes and Teresa would think about the two ends of the "Who am I as a woman?" spectrum that seem to gain the most attention where I live. On one end, the message "Let's be girl-boss-babes and crush the patriarchy by taking over the world" is strong. On the other end, the story is "Femininity over feminism—let's be Proverbs 31 women, here for hearth and home!" Both sides have their points to ponder, each side wags fingers at the other, and both have sharp barbs used as weapons against invisible enemies.

But neither reveals woman as she was fully designed to be.

Women wanting to be perfect in every way isn't a new idea at all. And the desire to crush the patriarchy isn't a new thing either.

I grew up singing "I am woman, hear me roar," and demanding equality at any cost.

Patriarchy is a real thing.

Matriarchy is a real thing.

Oppression is alive and well.

Prejudice is too.

I've held young women in Guatemala who were raped by family members. I've listened as moms in Jamaica shared stories of struggle to provide for their children after being abused and abandoned. I've walked the hallways of former Soviet complexes still used to house the elderly, addicted, and orphaned and watched the hopeful eyes of young women who hope to one day live an independent life. All they want is a fighting chance.

Patriarchy, matriarchy, oppression, and prejudice are legitimate challenges facing women. But they are not the true enemy. They can threaten. They can taunt. But as I watch you and me, I see a greater enemy.

The trouble with women is *us*.

Yes, it's us. It's the way we respond to the challenges. It's the way we treat ourselves. It's the way we treat womanhood and all that's associated with it. We mock our bodies, we deride getting older, we complain about parenting. We pit ourselves against other women in a battle for perfection. Instead of rising above the critique and believing ourselves to be truly made in the image and likeness of God and celebrating what makes us divinely unique, we get trapped in anger and find ourselves finger-pointing.

We point the finger at men (or women) and say, "It's their fault."

We point the finger at culture and say, "They make it way too hard."

We point the finger at systemic flaws in governments and entities and say, "There's no hope."

But the voice that's loudest in our heads is the voice of comparison, the voice of jealousy, the voice of self-deprecation and self-pity. It's the voice that slices away at our very DNA.

2

Let's Talk about You

I've lived a lot of life and am likely older than most of the folks who will read this book. And I watch friends post stories about what to prepare for in our forties, our fifties, and beyond. The articles shared are nearly always for women. In fact, doing a quick (and highly unscientific) Google search, I discovered that the number of articles for women addressing challenges associated with everything from success to dating to growing older is ten to one compared to those same types of articles for men.

The articles are written by women in cultures that place pressure on women to slay every day but never to age, never to change, never to evolve. They talk about those things as if they are enemies.

Everything takes a toll. The things we define as beautiful are stripped away. The things we define as powerful are weakened.

For Christians, the added pressure of the proverbial "Proverbs 31 woman" wraps itself around our necks. We must be industrious, brilliant, self-sufficient, creative, clever, never doubting, ever faithful, always optimistic. We'd better be married with a bustling household. It works in our great favor if we're chefs in the kitchen, funny at the dinner table, and fully capable of weaving the napkins everyone uses to wipe their mouths after eating the bread we baked and slathered with the butter we churned and are selling under an exclusive label at Trader Joe's. (Yes, I believe my butter would be happiest there because all their food is fun.)

Though she tries to be kind, the church often sounds like the culture she wants to redeem. We look for the right angle, the right words, the perfect positioning statement to gain the attention of the world. And we get confused about where women fit in that message. We argue about that Proverbs 31 woman—where she should live, what power she should be given, what authority she might have to make a difference or to lead, or whether she should even have a voice at all.

Scripture says we are made in the image and likeness of a God who has personality, emotion, imagination, intuition, wisdom, and creativity. I don't know if you noticed, but I began this section about design with Genesis 1. That's right. Before Genesis 2, there was you. God designed man and woman in His image and likeness, then said, "I've got big plans for you. I've poured everything I am into you. And this is so very good" (my paraphrase).

In Genesis 2, a bit more detail is offered about the "very good" moment, about a deep sleep and God's skilled hands shaping flesh and bone into new flesh and bone. When explaining why God would choose to use a rib to design a woman, many wax poetic about a woman being by a man's side and near his heart and under his arm. But before Genesis 2, there is Genesis 1. There is God forming and breathing, deliberate in His design of both man and woman to reflect His full image and likeness. They are designed with the same substance, the same breath, the same connection with creation. He looks at both of His masterpieces of design and calls them "very good." He blesses them.

He didn't merely form woman; He was purposeful in the word picture He chose to describe the creative moment. You see, ribs guard the heart and lungs. Ribs give strength to stand. Life can be sustained without many bones in the body, but life cannot be sustained without a ribcage. Ribs are flexible, able to expand and contract as needed to create space for breath. It's only when those ribs are broken that they become a danger to the very life they are designed to protect.

The phrase that refers to the woman in Genesis 2 is *ezer kenegdo*. Translated, it means "helper of the same nature" or "strong helper standing face-to-face."[1] Think about the weight of each of those words. Strong. Helper. Standing. Face-to-face.

We are created in strength to actively contribute to and provide what is necessary, ever upright and powerful, and always rich in relationship.

I don't know about you, but I read those words and know how often I've not believed them to be true. I've denied my divine heritage. I've not seen myself as having God-designed strength. I've judged myself by a list of tasks rather than seeing my *self* as the real contribution to the restoration of the world around me.

And when you and I don't see ourselves rightly, self-condemnation can torment us. *Everyone else . . . If only . . . You can't because . . .* become whispers that sound like screams.

Lourdes and Teresa didn't listen to the lies, and I'm so thankful.

Your Beautiful Design

So what makes up that unique, God-crafted design found within you and me?

The way our eyes focus and perceive is different from the way men's eyes work. Our rods and cones—the photoreceptors in our eyes that communicate what we see—provide more clarity and definition in the way we see and how much we see. Where men see color, we see nuance within the color.[2] And the old adage "A mom has eyes in the back of her head" may not be so far off. Research has shown that many women have wider peripheral vision than men—up to 180 degrees around them. The wider vision arc allows a woman to take in a greater amount of information without moving her head.[3]

Those ears of yours are also uniquely wired. You are more adept at distinguishing and categorizing sounds—even multiple sounds coming from different locations at the same time. In the same way your eyes perceive nuance, so do your ears. Sound isn't isolated; rather, small changes in tone or pitch are not just heard by us but *felt*. While what we feel isn't always spot-on, we do indeed feel an emotional connection within what we hear.[4]

Maybe you feel that connection because, as a woman, your nervous system is more finely tuned. You sense connection more quickly, feel the environment in addition to taking note of your surroundings.[5] Some folks call it a woman's intuition, but DNA says it's your brain's amazing ability to switch back and forth between facts and feelings because its two hemispheres have more connectors than the brains of men.[6] Our brains also help us remember more and have stronger verbal, reading, and writing skills.[7]

There are more beautifully designed DNA differences within you, from the way you make decisions and process emotional experiences to the way your brain ages. But there's more to your design than DNA. Much more.

Deeper than DNA

From the beginning, women have played a pivotal role in Scripture. Again, "strong helper standing face-to-face" was hand shaped and designed by a God who said, "This is very good." In the pages of the Bible are judges, prophets, teachers, leaders of countries, apostles, healers—all women. Women asked the hard questions. Women took the risks. Women read the room and sounded the alarm.

Lydia became a role model because of her success in business and her commitment to serving others (Acts 16:11–15).

The daughters of Zelophehad stood up to lawmakers to negotiate for the rights to their father's land (Num. 27:1–11).

Shiphrah and Puah thwarted the plans of the Egyptians and saved a new generation of Israelites—all without raising their fists or their voices (Exod. 1:8–21).

Women were always active in Christ's ministry too. He treated them with dignity, included them in the work of the gospel, loved them fully. He understood the rejection felt by the woman at the well and stayed with her for two days as she boldly preached to the men in her village (John 4:1–42), and He celebrated the gumption of the Canaanite woman (Matt. 15:21–28). He moved a woman twisted in pain to the center of the temple, where her female ancestors had once been free to worship. And in front of everyone, He smiled and said, "Woman you're free!" (Luke 13:10–17). He adored Martha and Mary, two sisters who were front and center in His public ministry and personal life (Luke 10:38–42).

And on the morning of His resurrection, it was the women who showed up first (Luke 24:1–2). Mary Magdalene. Mary. Joanna. The resurrection story is incomplete without them. Their presence and participation remains a powerful reminder that women were never also-rans or second thoughts. They remind us all that we are "strong helper standing face-to-face."

Throughout His ministry on earth, Jesus selected women who were unafraid of stepping into life by passing through death. He chose the ones who were willing to simply show up. They were bold and fierce and unafraid to risk for the sake of the gospel. They were unafraid to let go and embrace faith. They were willing to carry the load and walk unknown paths.

They were willing to weep at the cross and walk before dawn— while the rest of the world slept.

It was these women who changed the world then. Mary, Mary, and Joanna celebrated Jesus's resurrection and soon were counted in the 120 who awaited the power of Pentecost to fall like rain in an upper room. Married. Single. Old. Young. Wealthy. Impoverished. Aristocrat. Commoner. Since the beginning, women have been purposeful. They have been powerful. And there's even more that's woven in us.

Proverbs 31 is most often quoted as a twenty-two-verse homage to wives, moms, and grandmas. Rarely is the chapter read in its entirety. The chapter is written by King Lemuel, but the true author of the words is his mom. He calls the words inspired and strong. They begin with a lesson on leadership and a warning not to give away our affection to the things that destroy kingdoms. She encourages rest and restoration, loving well by leading well, giving a voice to the voiceless, and serving with palms up and knees bent as God's life is incarnated in ours.

And then she starts describing a picture of true leadership—a best-in-class example for her son to pursue.

We don't know the leader's name, but this we do know about her: she is trusted because her life is trustworthy. She's strong and industrious, always looking for ways to care for others—especially those who serve. She has no need to fight to be right because she does right daily. She looks at everything around her as an opportunity to care more wholly, and she is unafraid to dig in deep. She's wise in her financial decisions, responding with forethought in seasons of plenty to prepare for seasons of want, because she knows there will be both. She doesn't create chaos, and those she leads lack no good thing even in times of devastation. Her leadership lifts those around her and gives them places of honor. She invests time in people and finds joy when they benefit from that investment. She is unafraid of an uncertain future because she knows wisdom and kindness will greet her there—and they have not failed her yet.

And it's that same wisdom and kindness she shares with others. She knows that kindness attacks evil at its core, and she sets up guards around her words to ensure they are used for good. Again, she is trusted because she is trustworthy with the days that have been given to her.

At her core, the Proverbs 31 woman isn't an enviable wish list for the perfect wife and mom. No, this story is about a woman who leads and serves well. She knows she is counted on by family, friends, employees, and the community, so she starts her day by preparing for it, making sure it is placed on the right track by tending to the nourishment of her body, soul, and spirit. She ends her day by retreating to a quiet place—a sanctuary so valuable to her well-being that she has honored it by giving it the best she has.

There is speculation that the mom of King Lemuel was Bathsheba, a woman known more for scandal than leadership. There is more speculation that if Bathsheba was the author of the wisdom, it may have been Ruth she was describing. But when I read the words of King Lemuel, I can't help but think he sees Proverbs 31 in his own mom. He sees her investment, her commitment, her affirmation. He lauds her road-worthy wisdom. And the last two verses of the chapter are a celebration.

> Charm can be misleading, and beauty is vain and so quickly fades, but this virtuous woman lives in the wonder, awe, and fear of the Lord. She will be praised throughout eternity. So go ahead and give her the credit that is due, for she has become a radiant woman, and all her loving works of righteousness deserve to be admired at the gateways of every city! (vv. 30–31 TPT)

"She will be praised throughout eternity." We are *ezer kenegdo*, made in the image and likeness of God to celebrate His design in all we do. Out of all the voices clamoring for our attention, Proverbs 31 reminds us that it is the voice of praise that should ring loudest.

3

You Are Fierce and Exquisite

Lourdes and Teresa turned my world upside down as they simply embraced their God-given design. They saw themselves as active contributors in restoration. They walked in the wisdom of a mom of a king. And in doing so, they caused me to rethink what I believed—about leadership and service, about women, about myself.

Lourdes and Teresa were the beginning of my journey with women who taught me that God's purpose in us is real and true, even when our worth is questioned. They taught me that our lives are purposeful, even if they are quiet. In fact, some of the most powerful women I've learned from—women like the sisters, who believe restoration is a reality on earth as it is in heaven—are moving mountains with faith-filled whispers. Those whispers are significant, even if you or I never hear them. We feel their impact as the world is changed.

My mom would have loved the tenacity of Lourdes and Teresa, the savvy of Lydia, and the sass of the daughters of Zelophehad. She wanted me to be fierce, but she was the one who found true fierceness in her later years.

"How I Forgot to Be Who God Had Planned for Me to Be—and My Struggle Back to Reality." These words were written at the beginning of a seventeen-page testimony my mom penned in October 1999—just four short months before she died from the ravages of breast and bone cancer. The story was tucked in a brown envelope in a nondescript binder of poetry. The simple dedication at the front read, "To Ronne, with love, from MOM." One morning as I rummaged through some boxes in a closet looking for God knows what, I found it. I had read the poetry but had never opened the envelope.

That morning a friend had made a confession on Facebook. She said that the fear of not measuring up to others threatened to paralyze her—and the fear of not being pretty enough held her hostage. I quickly responded with encouraging words, sharing my own past demons of inadequacy that had screamed their loudest during the days when I'd modeled professionally.

Every monthly weigh-in determined whether or not I would get bookings. My business card featured not only my name but also my measurements and height. Every modeling gig paid bills and put food in my son's belly—essentials for an older, second-try collegiate single mom who was the sole provider. But the pressure to look beautiful took a damaging toll on my self-esteem.

The voices aren't as loud as they used to be, but they can still threaten to overwhelm me. I embrace the wrinkles that reveal where laughter has lived but shudder every time I put on a swimsuit and see the legs that lost their firmness due to bulimia. While styling my hair I roll my eyes when I see the silver-gray reminders of time that is passing far more quickly than I would have ever imagined.

In the media, I see countless images of women with nary a sag nor a wrinkle. The push for perfection is strong, no matter our age or stage of life. And the pressure goes deeper than physical flawlessness. The voices want me to believe I will be passed over in favor of those who are younger, brighter, smarter, cooler, more spiritual, more talented, more anything other than me because who would really want me.

Yes, those voices are there—the voices that want me to forget how to be who God has planned for me to be.

Those voices spoke to my mom too. For years, she carried the anger and sorrow of a life she felt was far from the life she should have lived. She wrote about that life in the beginning of her testimony. "I knew how to be glamorous and act brilliant about most everything. I could dress in my great-looking gowns, and because most people thought I was good-looking, I could stand with the best of them. . . . The greater I got at playing the part of someone else, the more fearful I became. I was dying inside."

The voices quieted about six months after my dad passed away. She recounted the story often, of being tucked away in her bedroom, angrily listing off the misfortunes of her life to God. "And then I heard a voice. It was so real. And that voice said, 'Wanda, I need you to sit down and be quiet. I've got some things to tell you.' So that's what I did. I got on my knees and I listened."

What proceeded was the love of a Father for His own. God told my mom she was talented and needed. He told her she was funny and a good listener. He told her He was proud of the way she cared for her family and that He didn't mind that she didn't drive a car. And He told her there was still lots of *life* left in her. That's when, for the first time, Mom embraced the true beauty of her gifts, her talents, her personality. Embracing God's design became the reality she walked out as she lived the last years of her life, a widow caring for and feeding others as an in-home healthcare provider (something she didn't think had any real value when she did it as a homemaker).

"It's all right for me to be the person that God created me to be. It doesn't matter what anyone else thinks. This is my gift from God and I will be that person. . . . The greatest thing that you could ever do in this life is *to be what God has already made you to be*. To build cities is a great thing. But maybe the greatest thing ever is to just be yourself. . . . To close your ears to that reality is like denying life itself."

Certainly, the "God knows what I was searching for" was really the "God knows exactly what I needed" that day back in 2013. I had been on the journey of reclaiming His divine design of women for only a short season, and reading my mom's words encouraged me to stay the course, to celebrate my God-given gifts of leadership, teaching, exhortation, and wisdom—and let my personality shine through the talents He offered. For Mom, those talents reflected His mercy as she tended to and fed those who couldn't care for themselves. For me, a talent for writing and gifts of exhortation and teaching allowed me to pour into stories of redemption—and find my own redemption in the process.

Yes, I am fierce. So are you. We are "strong helper standing face-to-face."

Say that out loud: "I am strong helper standing face-to-face—and my design is exquisite."

It's not a degree or a pedigree that defines you. It's an image and a likeness. You are fearfully and wonderfully made, even when told you are not enough. Right now you are fierce. Decades from now you will be fierce still. You are a masterpiece, despite challenges or brokenness or things called "weak." And you are exquisite.

Lourdes and Teresa, Ena and Pam, Dacia and Irene, Lilly and Lucy, Flo, Miss Mary, Lisa and Bianca, Elizabeth and Aunty, and Elena—the women whose stories fill these pages—are all exquisite too.

PART 2

RECLAIMING YOUR PURPOSE

The body of Christ misses out when we attempt to force all women into one constrained understanding of the role and responsibilities of women. Christ's transformation does not mean we blindly do as other good and godly people say we should. If we are simply content to go along just to get along, we will never come to realize our true purpose in life.

from "God Calls All Women" by Natasha Sistrunk Robinson, author and founder of Mentor for Life

> She's skilled in the crafts of home and hearth,
>   diligent in homemaking.
> She's quick to assist anyone in need,
>   reaches out to help the poor.
>
> Proverbs 31:19–20

4

God Is Not a Jerk

For a few years now, I've had an ongoing conversation on Facebook Messenger and WhatsApp. Call it mentorship, call it friendship, call it a unique pseudo-kinship relationship, but whatever you want to call it, the twenty-five-year-old in India and I have savored it for a long while.

We met in a Facebook group that focused on goal setting and productivity, and our talks have run the gamut from *Bajrangi Bhai-jaan* (one of the coolest movies I've ever seen) to the best worship songs, from why therapy costs so much in the United States to who pays for what at Indian weddings. He's taught me a lot about the inherent cultural pressures on young adults in India to do well in school and succeed quickly in business. His beyond-his-years questions have put my brain to shame a number of times.

He calls me Aunty—a term of endearment for an older woman who offers advice and care. We've argued, prayed, and had deep discussions about life. He says he doesn't understand why I put up with him. I say I don't understand why he relies on the clumsy wisdom of a suburban white woman from the United States.

Our relationship is just the kind Jesus loves.

The main topic of conversation that keeps emerging in the years-long message thread is "How will I know God's will for my life? How do I know what He wants me to do with my career, with my family, with a future spouse?" My friend gets trapped in the fear that he will miss God's great plan by *this much* and be forever regretful of a life that could have been amazing but ended up being just okay. He asks me for wisdom. I share what I've learned in this life as a follower of Jesus. God is always faithful to teach us both in the process.

My friend knows all about this book. He is confident that it's God's will. I, on the other hand, know all the "inside feelings" I battle—the ego that rises and the worry that emerges and the wondering that takes place. What happens if things fail or I fall? My friend thinks I've got it all figured out by now. But fear still wants to have its way with me.

Fear loves to write the story lines of our lives. It loves to scribble over our plans, edit our futures, add to our pasts, discredit our present journeys. And fear doesn't know how to write a good story, because fear can't spell *hope*.

Fear has whispered in my ear more than once that I will most certainly come to ruin, that the publishing company will soon realize the error of its ways and these words will not be worthy to be read. Age creeps into the story too—a haunting plotline that says I will cross over into the world of "too old to matter" and no one will deem me useful.

But here's the truth: God's will is not the smallest dot on a mystical bull's-eye that must be hit with laser accuracy in order for your life to matter. His will is not a deep-dive mystery that is passed out in puzzle pieces. And He is not a jerk who dangles a carrot in front of your hungry soul while He holds a baseball bat behind His back, ready to thwack you if you don't use pretty words to ask first or chew with your mouth closed.

Romans 12 lays out a beautiful guide to His will for each of us:

> So here's what I want you to do, God helping you: Take your ev-
> eryday, ordinary life—your sleeping, eating, going-to-work, and

walking-around life—and place it before God as an offering. Embracing what God does for you is the best thing you can do for him. Don't become so well-adjusted to your culture that you fit into it without even thinking. Instead, fix your attention on God. You'll be changed from the inside out. (vv. 1–2)

The more time I spend with women who not only see themselves as purposefully handcrafted in the image and likeness of God but also want to allow that design to be front and center in the way they view life and the way they lead and serve others, the more I see God's will as being as expansive and creative as He is.

5

Ena and Pam

Start with What You Have

My friend Ena lives the life described in Romans 12 well. She says, "I've always heard God tell me, 'Start with what you have. Put your feet in the water and see if the water parts in front of you.'"

A smart businesswoman, Ena owns a mission house for wayfaring strangers who travel to her country to care for the poor and discarded. The beds are comfortable, the food is hearty, and the mornings come to life with the sound of burro-bray alarm clocks and a milk truck that plays a most delightful song ending with "Mooooo!"

The mission house she opened to guests was originally the home in which she raised her family, until the kids grew up and moved away and her marriage crumbled around her. People she had met when she and her family lived in the United States for a few years asked if they might come to her Honduran village to do mission work. They said they would purchase some bunk beds if she'd open her home. Ena thought it sounded like a kind gesture, and the company would be nice.

Above all, Ena loved being a mom. She reminisced often about homeschooling her own children when they were young, and how Sundays were all-day celebrations at church. She felt a bit like a mom again when mission teams visited, resting on the wraparound stone porch filled with hammocks and comfy chairs. She loved how her two Chihuahuas always made themselves at home in the laps of guests who listened for that milk truck as the mornings washed the sky with yellow and pink and blue.

But as she watched the mission teams serve her community, Ena began feeling a nudge to do something more.

Ena believes that the God who created her knows without wavering that His is a powerful bloodline with a strong heritage and an even stronger future. God's purpose isn't that you figure out what He wants you to do with your life. His purpose is *you*. He created you because He finds delight in watching you breathe and respond and wonder and explore. He loves the way you love along the way.

When Ena felt the nudge to do something more, she wasn't looking for God's perfect will. She wasn't trying to figure out His great purpose. Ena simply missed homeschooling. She longed to teach again. She just wanted to do what she loved to do.

No Question but to Respond

Now, if titles and success were indicators of God's perfect will, then Pam had every reason to brag about being smack-dab in the center of His plan. She was vice president of marketing at a mobile technology company. She and her husband had the perfect home in the perfect neighborhood, and her auburn hair and big smile were the perfect accessories for her Mercedes. They attended a great church, were actively involved in their small group, and were raising their daughter to embrace all the goodness of a good, good Father.

"We had one child, and medically we couldn't have any more," she shared as she thought about the road that had taken them from perfectly manicured suburbia to a plot of land in remote Georgia—land filled with chicken coops and an old hunting shack tucked in gnarly trees. "We had always been interested in adoption but hadn't pursued it. Then I turned on the television one night and watched a show on PBS about the Heart Gallery, where photographers volunteer their time to take photos of foster kids. That was the first time I had ever heard that you could adopt kids right out of the foster care system. I went out to the garage and told my husband. He looked at me and without even a pause said, 'Let's do it.' It wasn't some big calling. It was just that simple."

Pam and her husband dove headfirst into training to make their home foster kid ready, and they started hearing the stories of the kids. It was the teenagers' stories that cut like a knife. "These older teenagers could turn eighteen and never have a family. One family's adoption didn't go through with a fifteen-year-old girl, and my husband said—totally out of the blue—'Call them and we'll take her.' Two weeks later, she was on our doorstep."

One daughter became two became eight. All but two were teens at the time they joined the family. Pam's picture-perfect world was transformed into a whirling dervish of makeup trends and crushes and growing-up drama and navigating life as lives rejected became lives redeemed.

"My dad wasn't my biological dad," Pam reflected. "But gosh, he loved me, and I loved him with all my heart. It's the hardest thing to watch people who don't know the level of their own belonging. When my husband and I encountered that level of brokenness, for us, there was no question but to respond."

Both Ena and Pam felt a nudge to do something. Neither woman agonized much about knowing God's perfect will before they took action. Instead, they simply trusted Him and responded.

6

Embracing Purpose

I wonder what it was like to be the first. I've been the first before in some things: the first person to hold a specific job title in an organization, the first person to speak on a roster at a conference, the first person to raise my hand in a classroom.

But I can't imagine what it was like to be Dorcas. Her story of being "first" is a powerful one.

Dorcas was the first Greek woman to be mentioned in Scripture for following Jesus (Acts 9:36–42). I love the cross-cultural welcome the author provides in Scripture as he shares her name first in Hebrew and then in Greek. Dorcas lived in the town of Joppa, and it's not known how she learned about Christ or why her heart stumbled toward His with such joy. That joy was inescapable. It moved her soul, her feet, her hands.

Dorcas was born a maker of things, and her creativity was saturated with color when Love found her. And so she wove fabric and made clothing and delighted in outfitting the poor. She knew her hands could do good because her heart had found its good. To those with need, she was an answer to prayer. And to those who wondered if they had any gifts to offer a King, she was a reminder that all gifts shine when seen through the prism of love—even gifts involving looms and needles and thread.

She had no kin with her when she died, and I wonder if they simply didn't exist or if they had walked away when she chose to follow Jesus. But God had crafted a family for her, and the widows of the town gathered to mourn, holding the clothing she had made. I imagine them saying, "There was something about her," as they wept. "She wasn't afraid to go first, to kneel first. She was the first to ask a beggar what he needed, the first to step in to help, the first to find a way."

Dorcas took God at His word when He said she was made to worship. She took Him at His word when He said He had woven her together and written a story within her. She took Him at His word when He said she was light and salt. She took Him at His word when He said her hands were crafted to do good things.

And so Dorcas became the first.

Her death became the first resurrection in the early church. Her raised-to-life-again story became the new-life story for others in her city. I can't help but think that if she were alive today, we would quickly elevate her, schedule a speaking tour for her, and sell tickets. We would have her share her secrets to a life worthy of resurrection and we would feverishly do our best to distill her words into viral-worthy quotes.

But Scripture tells us of no events like that. It simply says Dorcas's life of loving God and loving others changed lives for eternity. So I have a feeling that after being raised to life, Dorcas simply returned to doing what she loved to do, what she knew her hands could do.

Dorcas knew God's perfect will was simply that she live her life in His embrace. She was a maker. And she kept making.

Even the Leaders Will Follow

Filled with a desire to teach once again and encouraged by the work being done by mission teams in her community, Ena went to local schools looking for a place to volunteer as a tutor, and that's how she found La Invasion, a neighborhood built on the banks of a trash-filled river. Most of the families were squatters who were living on land they prayed they might someday own. In homes built from scraps, they hoped for the day there might be electricity and cool, clean water. Single moms worked the fields until dusk and then posted guard in their shanties so their children could rest. Meals were scarce, milk was a privilege, and water was a precious and costly gift purchased from large trucks that drove along the dirt roads every other week. The children in the community attended an overcrowded school with teachers who did their best. In fact, the principal had raised a bit of money to build a new schoolroom after the government had ignored pleas for help. Ena knew she had found a place for her feet to land. But the place needed far more than a volunteer tutor.

Ena went to the pastors of her church and told them about the neighborhood down the street from paved roads and comfortable homes. She told them about the children who struggled in school because their parents couldn't read and about the bellies that ached from a lack of food. "We always said we cared for the poor, and I knew they would want to help. Our church could volunteer there."

Their response was not what Ena expected to hear. "They told me that the neighborhood was not near the church and that they needed to focus on other things." Her heart sank, but she refused to walk away from the neighborhood she had found. Another woman at church, Esmerelda, shared Ena's passion for children, and the two women visited La Invasion and talked about what the future might hold. Along the way, they met other women who also wanted to help. They found a tiny two-room house in the neighborhood, and the women brought straw mats and a little food and set about offering care in the afternoons.

Using what they had in their homes, the women started Niños~Comunidad (NiCo). Afternoons were filled with children gathering to learn from a team of faithful volunteers. They received help with homework, lessons on health and hygiene, and a nutritious snack to strengthen their minds and bodies. And they were taught about their value and worth.

The school principal and teachers embraced the help, encouraging parents to let their children attend the tutoring sessions. Ena remembers what it was like those first years with the children. "It was shocking for me to see that kids in third grade were at a preschool level. They didn't even know their ABCs, they didn't even know their numbers, they didn't even know how to write their names. Even if they came for just some food, that was good enough for me, because then they would receive the Word of God, they would get some help with their schooling, and then they would get their meal."

In 2015, Orphan Outreach joined hands with Ena and Esmerelda as a ministry partner. It was an answer to Ena's prayers. "NiCo is a place of refuge for those kids who don't have a place to do homework or somebody who can help them with homework and someone who can give them a hug. They don't have those things at home, so NiCo is that—it's like their extra home. And I'm so thankful; honestly, I'm so thankful that God brought Orphan Outreach because now I can see that this will continue." NiCo initially provided care for struggling students in first through third grade, but over time it has grown to include classes for fourth through sixth graders and an early development program for kindergartners.

Ena could have waited on the government to provide care. She could have waited on pastors. She could have waited on anyone else. But instead, she embraced God's purpose. "If we wait for leaders to make a move, we could be waiting forever. We need to be unafraid to step out and do something. We can do it first, and then others—even the leaders—will follow."

One morning as we sat on her porch, she asked me to pray with her. "I really would like you to pray for somebody that has a heart to work with the moms. I have been praying for that, and I think now is the time when God is going to send that person to help us, to disciple the moms."

Ena has watched everything unfold at NiCo, and that prayer prayed years ago is now being answered. Ena herself has been feeling a new nudge to offer discipleship and job-skills training to women in the village. Yes, the answer to the prayer is Ena. "I'm not sure how it will all come about, but I'm again trusting God, and I hear Him saying, 'Ena, you know what to do. Start with what you have. Put that toe in the water.'" She laughed. "Oh my. It's all an adventure, isn't it?"

Ready or Not

When she watched the Heart Gallery documentary on PBS, Pam had no idea the trajectory her life would take. But she took one step after another as the days unfolded, and the bedrooms in her home were soon filled with teenage girls. There were dating relationships and heartbreaks and marriages and babies, decisions about education and careers and faith and friendships. Folks asked for advice, and soon Pam was writing a book, and then two, about the hard questions to ask when considering adoption and foster care and the things to remember when parenting kids from difficult backgrounds.

She aptly titled the series of books Ready or Not, and while they're packed with real-world, faith-filled advice and prayers, what makes them truly special is that they're glimpses into a life full of next-step moments.

Pam encountered countless foster children who missed the opportunity to have a family in their teen years. Another conversation with her husband became another next step—this time to found Connections Homes, a nonprofit committed to providing care for young adults struggling to transition from foster care into adulthood.

Pam knew how to tell stories, but launching a ministry was unknown territory. Tirelessly, she repeated the stories of what happens to our hearts and minds when we belong, what happens to our lives when we are given a place at the table. One by one, people began stepping forward to volunteer as mentors. "From the beginning, it's never been about asking people to become parents to these kids. Not everyone is called to adopt. Not everyone is called to foster. But we're all called to be family. We all want to know there's a safe place to ask questions about an apartment lease or if a résumé looks good or why friends flake out sometimes. It's good for us to have someone who's walked the road a bit longer than we have, someone who can help us make better choices. We just want to know we're not alone in this world."

Pam remembered the impact in her own life when someone stepped in and said, "I'll walk this road with you." And her commitment grew to make sure young adults aging out of foster care had the opportunity to hear those same words.

7

God's Purpose Is You

The first time Ena impacted my life I was not walking the dirt roads of La Invasion, the squatter community in her hometown. Instead, I was at the city hall down the street from my home in the Hill Country of Texas. I bundled up excitement and fear and walked them both into a booth, where I voiced my opinion with the turn of a dial and the click of a button. I've always known that voting for laws and leaders is not just a right but an honor. I've watched what happens when democracy is threatened in other countries, and I've seen the impact when there is no liberty at all.

So I voted that day. I made a choice based on what I believe in my heart is the right way to treat people. I made a choice based on who I say God is and my faith in what He can do—rather than what a person or a party can do. I walked into the booth, and I voted for people over leaders, because at the end of the day, it's people who care for people. God's will is this: that we love Him, and we love people.

And as I voted, I thought about Ena and how she hasn't waited on people in positions of power to influence change or make a difference. Instead, she simply does the right thing. She votes with her life. And it's people who win.

■ ■ ■ ■

I experienced the impact of Pam's story while sitting with her under the stars, watching her cats maneuver the porch railing while she shared a testimonial video her team had produced for a celebration and fund-raiser. "That's what this life is, after all. We try to box God in, to make Him tell us exactly what it is we're supposed to do. But life isn't a big, on-your-knees, mountaintop moment where God spells it all out in advance. We wouldn't know what to do with that. He knows that our trust comes in the day-to-day, facing the good and the hard and the surprising, making small choices along the way. His will is simply that we trust and obey. It's not any more complicated than that."

Pam speaks at conferences and teaches communities how to care for young adults, but she's also learning how to raise chickens. She and her husband moved from the comforts of the city to a farmhouse set back from a winding country road. They now live in a ranch home with one of the most comfortable guest bedrooms around. "This was always a dream of ours," she told me. "To one day have a place where our Great Pyrenees pup could play and our grandbabies could get messy. So much has changed in our lives, but really, nothing has. I'm still a woman passionately in love with Jesus, still a wife and a mom. I'll always be a champion for mentoring, but I wonder if there might be a day when a new dream emerges. I know God will be there when it does."

Emily P. Freeman's podcast, *The Next Right Thing*, is filled with gold nuggets about living a life with our eyes lifted in faith to God and our steps paced by trust in Him. One of my favorite quotes, from episode 76, is this: "God won't let you miss your own future."[1]

God promises us time and time again in Scripture that He is faithful. He says He will never leave us, that no one can snatch us from His hand, that every wonderful thing He designed within us will come to life through us because He doesn't simply start things and then walk away from them.

The more time I spend with women like Ena and Pam, the more I see God's will as creative and imaginative, just like He is.

It doesn't rob us of choice but rather gives those choices an opportunity to be life-giving. We make our plans and do our things and say a prayer and then just walk by faith. We don't get big, clear, booming words from God most of the time. *We just take the next step.* The good and rough and mundane moments are all there, wrapped up in whatever's happening in our lives. And through it all, God's right beside us proving His care, proving His power, proving His fidelity.

I think about the Sunday morning I spent under a bridge in downtown Austin. The smells of dust and city and cigarettes mingled with warm vanilla lotion from the bold embraces of the homeless who gathered for church and a good meal. As a ragtag band played an old hymn, I watched a woman dance with abandon—her long braids keeping time with the clothing that draped her frail, weathered body. She looked at me and nodded knowingly and then said, "Watch out, because God is speaking. This is where it's good, honey. This is where it's powerful."

She had no well-appointed place to hang pictures or curl up on a sofa. Her home was on wheels beside her—a shopping cart filled with blankets, some plastic bags and cardboard, a flashlight, and playing cards. And yet she felt safe in the community that gathered with her to sing praises and eat good fried chicken. She wasn't agonizing over God's perfect will for her life. Instead, she was savoring the days she had been given, basking in the affection she felt from a heavenly Father who thought enough of her to give her another day to breathe. Her purpose was found in His goodness to her. I never knew her name, but to this day when I think of her, I can't help but sway.

Our purpose isn't found in the "when I get it all together" or "when everything falls into place." It's not even an ultimate destination—any more than brokenness is. Both are just small dots on a map to glory, passing places like, "Gathering Up" and "Letting Go" and "Humbly Yielding" and "Fearfully and Wonderfully Made." "Perfect Job" and "Everything I Want" are nowhere to be found; "Perfect Father" and "All I Need" are.

People have written hundreds of articles about life not being truly fulfilling until we find the *one* thing we are supposed to do. Here's the truth. I'm not sure God has only *one* thing for each of us to do. I think His story is bigger than our small imaginations. I think His will is about what we do with the time we're given here on earth—what we do with the days we're given.

I'll say it again.

God's purpose for your life is bigger than you think. His will isn't an obscure road sign on a dark highway. His purpose is *you*, and His will is for you to live your life fully, no matter where that life takes you. His purpose isn't wrapped up in the *one* job or the *one* person or the *one* place. It's wrapped up in you.

I wrote this note to my wonderful friend from India one evening. I've gone back and read the words a time or two myself. "He created you because He actually thought you might enjoy it here, that you might gain something from the time you've been given. He created you because He thought you might like how it feels to be known and loved. He created you because He thought you might simply want to be here with Him—for now and for eternity."

Not too long ago, I received a message from that friend. "I'm sending you a voice message on WhatsApp because Facebook only allows one-minute ones. And, Aunty, there's one more thing that's not on the voice message. I'm writing a book. There's so much I've learned in the past four years of frantic searching and worrying and talking to people. I can either call it a waste or make something of it. Worst case, I've documented my years in a great way. Best, I'm helping who knows how many people like me." That's right, the young man who wondered how to be in God's perfect will is now taking a next step in the liberty of His greater purpose.

There's liberty in embracing the freedom God's will gives us to explore and wonder and take next step after next step. Certainly, it would be easier for God to determine one purpose for each of our lives, yet He adores us so much that He invites us to walk beside Him with all our hopes and dreams. He surprises us with opportunities, and He assures us with His promise that He is not going to leave us hanging. His delight is now what it was in the beginning—walking with us in the cool of the afternoon, having a great conversation. He spoke stars into existence, and He purposed them to shine for us.

That's because His purpose is us. His purpose is *you.*

PART 3

RECLAIMING YOUR SHAPE

You don't have to have the last word. You don't have to prove your side. You don't have to wait for the truth to reveal itself—just live. Just live your life and trust that what happened existed to prepare you for what is next. And then, wait with breathless anticipation about what's coming. Because I promise, it will be beautiful.

from an Instagram post by Elora Ramirez,
story coach and editor

She's like a trading ship that sails to faraway places
and brings back exotic surprises.

Proverbs 31:14

8

"And In Itself And"

I've always had a fascination with ampersands. If we walked upstairs to my office (which would also be the place you would stay if you were visiting), you'd find a collection of them. I like the full-on, filled-with-curves-and-flourishes ampersands and spent hours practicing them on paper the same way some kids practice multiplication tables. I think they're beautiful, and not just because they look poetic on a page. Ampersands are unique in their purpose. The word actually stands for "and in itself and." Ampersands marry two things without diminishing the value of either. When I think of that definition, I see an ampersand as not simply additive but also inclusionary.

Though the sentiment of many in our culture is that you and I should find and focus on the *one* thing we are going to do, the women who are quietly and gracefully changing the world around them are living lives that look far more like an ampersand than a period. In fact, I believe that God is the God of the ampersand.

I first saw that image of Him on a spring day in Guatemala a few years ago. Courtney and I had been in the country for a couple weeks, working at children's homes and in community programs. It was our final day of ministry in the country, and the mission team we were leading had gathered in the lobby of the little hotel that had become our home away from home. Suddenly, Courtney's countenance changed. She shot a darting glance at me and then ran out the front door. In the lobby, casual conversation became concerned questioning.

Courtney was the one who always stood resilient, the one who always comforted others, the one who always had the words for me when my own voice was gone. She was the only one who was unafraid to stick with me when I was spiraling on the inside yet putting on a strong face for everyone on the outside.

I ran out of the hotel and found her under a grove of trees, doubled over, fists clenched, and ready to battle an invisible enemy. "I can't do this," she sobbed. "This is too much. He's going to make me give it all up—that's how He is."

"Who's going to make you give *what* up, Court?" I asked. "You're not making sense. Did someone call you? Is something going on back home?"

Her eyes darkened as she looked at me. "God is going to make me walk away from what I love. That's how He is. He makes us choose the one thing. We're supposed to do the one thing well."

The pieces started falling into place. Back in Texas, paperwork waited that would give the final nod for Courtney and her husband to pursue adoption through foster care. It had been a long and prayerful road for them, a road born from one of our first mission trips to Guatemala together, the country that had become her second home.

Most days she was thrilled about the opportunity. But this day she was crushed, because this day she felt the weight of choosing—the weight of the "or." This wasn't a choose-good-over-evil or a do-right-over-wrong choice. This was beauty for beauty. In a world and a culture that tell us we need to focus on doing one thing well, she had been given a glimpse of a future that suddenly caused her to believe she would have no choice but to sacrifice her present. On that hard-pressing morning, she felt God saying, "Give your present-day love to Me." And she heard another voice hiss, "And He'll never give it back."

Standing beside my friend as she wept and raged, I heard that voice too, because the hope of the future can darken even the brightest goodness of the present, pitting the two like enemies. My fumbling, frail trust in the Creator who imagined me, handcrafted me, and embossed His hands with my name was exposed that morning—for I saw Him as one too weak, too limited, too small to carry more than one delight for His own.

The same hissing voice was there for me that day. "Certainly, your God demands only sacrifice."

I doubted the very words that tumbled out of my mouth in response. "What if He's not making you choose at all?" I asked.

"You don't understand," she sobbed. "When our child moves in, that's it. That will be our life. There won't be any more serving in Guatemala or anywhere for that matter. This season will be done. Forever."

The words kept tumbling. "What if, just maybe, He's going to show Himself to be a both/and God instead of an either/or guy? Who says doing something new means what you're doing right now is dead? The Bible says He enlarges our space—maybe that means He gives us room to hold more."

There was silence as we held each other. And in the moment, there was a little glimmer of hope that the God who doesn't stand back and watch us struggle to hit His will on a small target just might be the same God who has something bigger in store for us than a do-only-one-thing life.

9

Dacia and Irene

A woman's body is a fascinating thing. It bends and moves and adapts to creation. I've been with women in developing villages who carry babies on their backs as they balance firewood on their heads and hold the hands of the elderly as they walk miles to fetch water. I think there's a greater story to be told in the strength of our shoulders and the way our hips curve just so and how we instinctively cradle an infant to hear the quiet beat of our hearts. I believe we are living, breathing ampersands, designed for inclusion.

Now, I'm not in the "Woman, you can do it *all*!" camp that can exhaust a soul. But I believe that the seasons of our lives are inclusionary—that God delights in adding ampersand after ampersand to our journeys as we move from season to season. Nothing is laid to waste, nothing is set aside. There is no "Choose one or the other, but you can't have both" or "Lay that thing down because it's now all about this thing." Instead, our souls bend and move and adapt as we shift the weight and find the heartbeat again.

Dacia laughed when I described the idea of the ampersand to her on the phone while talking about how her life was curving once more to fill the space of future days. We've known each other for more than a decade, and I've learned much from her as she's moved from Texas to Uganda and back again. "It's real, isn't it?" she said. "No one tells us that the new things we're doing are actually filled with the legacy of what came before. But it's true—and that makes our stories even more meaningful."

Dacia's story might be seen as more of a chapter book by casual observers. There's Dacia the pastor's child, who witnessed the cruelty of ministry as her dad was dismissed from his church and became a janitor for a season just to put food on the table; Dacia the spray-tanned Texan beauty, who had a plan for business success in the world of finance; Dacia the free-spirited soul, who sold everything but the spray-tan machine and her high heels and moved to Uganda to work at a children's home; Dacia the weary young wife and mom, who wondered if there would be any ministry waiting for her when she returned to the West Texas plains with her new family by her side; Dacia the minister to young women rescued from sexual exploitation and abuse.

From the first day I met her on a church patio in Austin, Texas, she's always been reluctant to say, "This is who I am." Rather, Dacia's words have always been, "This is what's being asked of me right now." She said, "I think God has to make ministry life feel all glamorous just to pique our curiosity. Then we take the plunge and say, 'Oh wait—what did we get ourselves into?'"

■ ■ ■ ■

I think if Dacia and Irene ever met, they would be best friends. Their lives are very different, and yet the bending and shaping that have taken place in them both reverberate with the ampersand story of God.

"When doctors in Guatemala tell you difficult news, their tone is always blunt and hard and to the point. There is never hope in their words," said Irene.

I first fell in love with Irene through pictures of the students she adores at the school she and her husband founded years ago. There are nearly fifty of them now, ranging from infants to adults.

Every day she fights for their freedom and their futures. She fights for their lives.

But that was never her plan.

Irene's life was settled. A pastor's wife in Guatemala City, she and her husband, Alfredo, had two lovely daughters who were thriving in elementary school. She was doing what she loved. So it comes as no shock that her world was rattled when a woman at their church looked at her and said, "I've been praying for you. God has told me you will have a son, and he will change the country."

Though she was taken aback, Irene smiled and graciously replied, "Oh, you must be mistaken. We have two daughters. We're good. No plans for any more children!"

Two years later, Irene heard the words, "Congratulations, you're pregnant again!" from her doctor. It was an unexpected and difficult season, and she was rushed to the hospital early to deliver the baby girl everyone was expecting.

They welcomed a precious baby boy instead.

Named Alfredo Jr., he was the shooting-star wish come true for a dad who always dreamt of having a namesake.

Within a few months, it was evident that something was wrong with Alfredo Jr. His development was delayed, and something was amiss with his heart. A visit to specialists and a battery of tests revealed that the infant boy had Down syndrome—and he needed heart surgery. The doctors delivered the news with no emotion and little hope. In Guatemala, the futures of children diagnosed with special needs weren't painted in bright tones. "Your son will always struggle," the doctor said. "He will never be able to really learn or hold a job or ever live on his own." Irene and Alfredo looked at their precious boy and then at each other. The doctor's words sounded like a death sentence.

Irene thought of the bold proclamation made by the woman at church years before. She shook her head, wondering how a boy who was unable to care for himself could change a country.

10

Shaped by Love

Irene and Dacia faced the fear. Courtney faced the fear. I know that fear. I've faced it too—the fear of *all the unknowns*. We're pretty good at facing fears we can name. Research shows that women are quick to rise from a knockdown and quick to rally when the odds are against us. But the unknown, unnamed fear? That is far more difficult to overcome.

We fear getting so close or growing so much only to fall or fail. We fear that everything good must end for the next thing to happen at all. We fear we won't have any right response—that nothing will be powerful enough, nothing will be profound enough, nothing will have lasting value.

It's often the unnamed fear that silently drives us to do all we can to make an impact, to find our place, to dig in our heels and stake our claim and stay the course. It tells us we're missing the mark if we aren't successfully pursuing the things God has purposed for us to do. It causes us to cling tightly to the present rather than to trust God with the journey. It keeps us from seeing all the ways our lives have thus far revealed God's inclusive design and all the bends yet to be formed that will benefit lives yet to be seen.

Yes, no matter where we find ourselves—new city, new job, new family, new life stage—God is ready to use our beautiful ampersand shape to help us gracefully serve and lead.

There Is No Nothing

I think about Naomi when I consider God's response to our fears. Yes, Naomi of the Old Testament, the mother-in-law faced with a new unknown. She saw only new in front of her—a new life that was washed with fear of *so many unknowns.*

Things had been going well for her. She had a beautiful life, a good family, and a future that looked bright. There were days in the sunshine, and there was the promise of big belly laughs and sticky toddler kisses and pet names like Nana or GiGi.

And then, piece by piece, that secure life started falling—shattering like painted tiles hitting a stone floor.

The man she vowed to love forever died. The sons she couldn't help but cherish died. And the woman whose name means "sweet" found herself all alone, held together only by people who shared little heritage and no DNA.

> Then she told them, "Don't call me Naomi any longer! Call me Mara, because God has made my life bitter. I had everything when I left, but the LORD has brought me back with nothing. How can you still call me Naomi, when God has turned against me and made my life so hard?" (Ruth 1:20–21 CEV)

Naomi's name no longer described her. She was not a wife or mom. Pain stripped the sweetness from the life she thought she would have.

She stood aching, wandering, lost. "Call me bitter," she said. The name was filled with meaning—a life that was difficult to swallow, a future unsure, a million questions with no good answers, hope overshadowed by dark day upon dark day. Naomi questioned whether there was any life left to live.

And yet when I read Scripture, I picture God calling her again by her real name—sweet. "I'm not going anywhere. I'm not leaving. I'm here beside you, and I'm going with you." Through Ruth's words and actions, I think Naomi was reminded of God's presence in her story. "We are in this together—in shadow and sunlight, in beauty and pain. And I believe there is still much life to be lived. Watch Me redeem this."

The fear of every unknown is overcome by the power of the God of the ampersand. He shapes every piece of our stories into something purposeful.

When Love Shapes a Story

Dacia's faith blossomed early. As a child, she saw God provide miraculously for her family. As a teen, she felt her faith come alive with dreams of doing some sort of local ministry. She wanted to be successful, and she wanted to honor the Lord in all her efforts. She had only one stipulation. "I said I never wanted to be a teacher or own a business. And I definitely didn't want to be a missionary or be on a church staff. I wanted ministry to be different—on my own terms. I still believed there was a sweet side to the body of Christ in the midst of pain, and I wanted to find that side."

Doing ministry on her own terms meant Dacia would walk away from the idea of ministry for years, focusing instead on a career and her community of friends. She lived in Dallas, Texas, and found herself swept away in the lifestyle of the city. The more deeply she plunged into debt, the greater the pull of ministry became to her. "I had no idea what ministry looked like for me, and I had no faith it could happen because of the chains my lifestyle had created."

And then Dacia fell in love.

She traveled to Uganda for ten days on an exploratory trip with a local church. She came home broken but didn't think she would return to the beautiful country. Yet she did, and it was after she returned from her second trip to Africa that I met her on that church patio—when she knew God was calling her to move. She sold everything and moved in with a family willing to open their home to her. Bit by bit she paid down her debt and found sponsors willing to support her as she packed her bags for the eighty-five hundred mile one-way journey.

But the decision to move didn't come easy for Dacia.

"Moving went against every grain in my soul. It was terrifying and exciting. Honestly, I was most concerned because I had no flats. I owned only wedges and heels. I wasn't missionary material. When I first arrived in Uganda, the missionaries there said, 'Oh, she'll never make it.' But I was determined not to lose *me* in the calling that God had for me. I was afraid I would disappear. I had to still be Dacia."

Dacia says she's heard God audibly only two times in her life. The first was on a plane returning from a Beth Moore conference soon after her second trip to Uganda. "As clearly as a bell, I heard Him tell me to sit between two women on a nearly empty plane. I rolled my eyes because it was such an idiotic thought. But I couldn't ignore it, so I finally plopped myself between the two women who both looked at me like I was crazy. By the end of the flight, I was crying and telling the women that I believed God was calling me to move to Uganda—and what an insane idea that was because I was so debt strapped. One of the women wrote out a check and handed it to me. God showed me He was serious about making a way."

A year into her journey, Dacia and I traveled those orange roads of Uganda together and breathed in the smoke and dust and smells of a world so far removed from the familiar. She had traded in her wedges for cute flats but still found joy in fingernail polish, colorful scarves, and the bangle bracelets that delighted the fifty-four children to whom she served as "Mama" at the Arise Africa baby home in the village of Bukaleba. Her spray-tan machine followed her on her journey, and she found a salon in nearby Jinja that offered lash extensions. She did what she could to remain the same Dacia she knew before she made the decision to take a step of faith and cheer for toddlers and weep for children found abandoned and abused in their mud and dung huts.

And then Dacia fell in love once more.

She was introduced to a tiny, malnourished infant, lost in a pile of blankets wrapped around her frail body on the front porch of the baby home. For two years, the two were inseparable. Dacia bent her body around the tiny girl at night and cradled her during the day. People questioned her ability to do ministry with a little one in tow. Dacia wondered if she would have to choose between serving one and serving many. She prayed God would give her the strength to do both.

And then, again, Dacia fell in love.

She wasn't expecting to meet anyone on the mission field; in fact, she was wrestling with the Lord over being content with singleness. It was the second time she heard God's audible voice, this time after a disastrous first date with a fellow missionary from the United States who was also serving in Uganda. Only a few weeks before, a friend had prayed she would find a good man. Then she met Josh. As Dacia threw herself down on her bed to weep after an evening when nothing seemed to go right, she heard God say, "Josh is the one." Dacia and Josh talked candidly about the changes both of them thought would come because of marriage and prayed for each other for those fears to be released. A year later, they were married. "God knew I needed to hear Him that first night, because the road isn't an easy one for us. We see so much and experience so much."

Josh loved Dacia, and he loved the little baby girl too. After they married, he started working for Arise Africa, and they began the process of adoption. Together they held the dying and went to battle for the weak. And Dacia learned that the first step taken is rarely the hardest step. It's the steps beyond that both test and strengthen our faith.

"I thought just packing my bags for Uganda and leaving my job, my red lipstick, and my high heels was living the uncomfortable life. Then I thought the hardest part would be not becoming numb to the hurt and poverty around me, not becoming callous to the pain. Then the hardest part became still trusting God with the decisions that seemed to reverse what it was I thought He wanted in my life."

Dacia returned to West Texas only two years after confidently saying, "Josh and I see ourselves in Uganda for the long road." Falling in love yet again moved both of them to consider walking away from the country that had become home and the people who had come to depend on them. A baby boy was on the way, and Dacia's heart ached for family. The unknowns of fear were familiar this time, and she was far more comfortable with the bending that was to come. "It might sound crazy to know that creature comfort won't be easy. I see my homeland now as a mission field and have to trust that God's providence is with us no matter where we are. Knowing what He's shaped in me so far is giving me hope for what He has in store."

While still in Uganda, Dacia launched a small online shop called Linger Boutique. She wanted to help women—especially young women—find hope and empowerment by offering up her profits for things like school tuition and mentoring. The shop stayed open after she moved back to the United States, and for a while, Dacia thought she might open a retail outlet where she could invite folks to hear the stories, have a cup of tea, and change lives with their purchases.

And as part of her pattern, Dacia fell in love. Again.

This time it was with the very women she hoped to help with her store. She heard about a ministry forming in West Texas that offered rescue and restoration to young women victimized by sexual abuse and exploitation. The ministry needed an executive director—someone with road-tested understanding and a passion to make a difference. The orange roads of Uganda were the catalyst for the next ampersand curve in Dacia's story.

And He Will Change the Country

It was love that shaped and bent Irene's life as well. The pastor's wife and mom to two beautiful daughters wrapped herself around the fragile baby boy deemed hopeless in her country.

"We went through such hard days, waiting patiently for someone to provide any good news. We were living in the process, trying to understand." She learned that heart defects affect almost half of all children born with Down syndrome. She learned Alfredo Jr. wasn't alone. There were other children out there like him. But where?

Heart surgery was essential, so little Alfredo was placed on the waiting list at San Juan de Dios, a children's hospital that serves all of Central America and the Caribbean. "Every time our baby boy was almost at the top of the list, something would happen, and Alfredo's name would be moved back down."

He was nearly two when the family received an invitation to travel to Wisconsin to see a heart specialist. Irene had no idea where Wisconsin was, and she was told to bring a coat—something she didn't own. What Irene found in the wintery, American state was not what she had expected. "It was there we learned about all the free services offered to parents of children with Down syndrome in the United States. We learned about what therapies are offered even to the youngest infants, and we found out there was tremendous support provided to families. I realized during that time that Down syndrome wasn't a bad thing at all."

Irene and Alfredo Sr. had learned that their son's heart condition was treatable by surgery—and that the best pediatric heart surgeon in the world lived in Guatemala City. "Healing Alfredo's heart may have been the urgent thing to ensure he lived, but helping him live well with Down's was the good thing—the thing that would change his life."

Irene's eyes had been opened to a world of possibility for her son and other children like him in Guatemala. She knew theirs wasn't the only family needing help. Story after story began to emerge of parents who struggled because their children with Down syndrome were provided no care from the Guatemalan government. The children were shunned and often treated poorly.

Her mother heart longed to do something for Alfredo and the other children. But what could she do in a country that held so little regard for the care of children with special needs? She wept and she prayed for a miracle. "I remember the day my husband looked at me and said, 'We can do something for families in our own country.' I told him, 'I believe we need to, but how? It takes money we don't have. We are not in a position to help.' He smiled at me and said, 'I know what we must do. We will sell our house to get the money.' I looked at him and said, 'If that's what you believe, that's what we will do. I trust you.'"

As little Alfredo recovered from open-heart surgery, Irene and her family boxed up their belongings. Their house sold quickly, and they used the money to launch Down Guatemala, a Christ-centered organization focused on providing educational resources, therapeutic care, and life-skills training to children and families affected by Down syndrome. Over a decade later, Irene often thinks about that night at the church when a woman told her she would have a son who would change Guatemala.

"A rabbi once told me, 'We believe two things about children: our kids choose their parents, and our kids choose how they will come to this earth. The Lord has given you a private teacher of love, faith, patience, and miracles.'" She has shared these words so many times, and still they get caught in her throat.

Down Guatemala offers far more than educational basics to students and therapeutic care and training to infants and their parents. The children are provided high-quality instruction based on their development level so that each student is given the greatest opportunity for success. Rarely does Irene have a conversation that isn't accompanied by students laughing and practicing language skills or working on a song and dance routine.

Students at the school are taught critical life skills, including cooking, managing finances, and even how to walk through difficult situations. When a student passed away, the teachers offered counseling and taught the children about the importance of grieving with hope.

Down Guatemala also partners with the Special Olympics; the Guatemalan Surfing, Golf, and Pool Associations; and area schools to create one of the most robust activity programs in the country. "Our kids get to golf on courses that are only open to the extremely wealthy. They are learning to swim and surf. They are spokespeople for the Special Olympics. And they will beat you every time at pool."

The newest shape taking form at Down Guatemala is the outreach being done in churches throughout the city. "If churches care for children, parents will feel safe attending church again," Irene said, thinking about how far things had come since she held her precious baby boy and wondered if he would have a future at all.

Irene and her family exemplify the beauty of a life lived amid the ampersand bends and twists. God yet again adding but also including.

11

God of the Ampersand

Yes, God is the God of the ampersand. He is the God of "Give me your child, and I will shape you for a nation." He is the God of "Give me your army, and I will shape you for victory." He is the God of "Give me your portion, and I will make you whole." He is the God of "Give me your life, and I will give you life lived fully."

On that morning under the trees in Guatemala, He reminded Courtney and me of His "and this too" heart. We prayed, held each other close, celebrated. Though we had no idea what His "and this too" might be, we believed He was kind enough to provide it.

That morning was six years ago. Courtney and her husband adopted Sylvia, a fiery teen with a heart for the poor and broken. Sylvia has become a teacher of culture and compassion. Now a missions pastor, Courtney continues to serve internationally, and her family joins her. And what she's learned through it all—the ministry and the adoption and the bending in trust—has opened the door for full-time ministry at home in Austin.

Courtney gave God her passion to care for the struggling in one country, and He bent her arms to hold the struggling daily in her own home *and* around the world.

Dacia gave God her love for the vulnerable, and He shaped her heart to bring restoration to them. All that she had learned

88

in Uganda, all that she had learned as a small business owner, all that she had learned in working with children who had been ravaged and trafficked, all that she had learned as a wife and a mom became the very things that shaped her perfectly to carry the burdens of young women in West Texas. Not one piece of Dacia's life was shelved to make room for another. No, the God of the ampersand knew her form, and He bent ministry and marriage and motherhood and merchanting into an inclusive shape.

"You don't have to move across the world to be uncomfortable," shared Dacia as she considered the curves her life had taken. "Sometimes it's a job change, it's doing something you said you could never do, it's trusting that He wants to take us beyond the safe harbor so we can see what He is capable of. Once you do, the safe harbor is where you go to be restored and refreshed, but you long to get back to the uncharted territory because there is nothing like it."

Irene gave God her days, and He gave her a country.

"This is God's mission—we've been doing this for what, ten years or so? Oh wow, I used to fight with God about the struggles. We wouldn't know where the money would come from, or we would be having challenges with the government, or I would just be so tired from working and caring for my family, and I would cry out, 'God, explain to me how this is going to work. You got us here. Now what are You doing?' And every time something happened. Always miracles. Always. I've learned. I don't fight anymore—I just say, 'God, You have this. You have us. Your will be done.'

"These kids don't have limits, you know," she quietly said as the noise of a spontaneous party grew around us. "We adults try to place limits on them, but they are limitless. They show me that God is not limited. He is always wanting to do something new in our lives.

"Our son has taught me how to love, how to be sincere, how to forgive and pray. He's taught us how to enjoy life. His friends may have difficult life stories, but they all enjoy life here. They have a different sight. They see life differently."

Differently. I wish this *differently* could be packaged and given to everyone, because this world desperately needs differently. This woman, this school, these students have given me hope that differently is possible.

Not one piece of your past will be wasted on your present. God is there, weaving purpose into every season. He is there, saying, "Test me in this, and see if I don't open up heaven itself to you and pour out blessings beyond your wildest dreams" (see Mal. 3:10).

I hear God say, "Come expectant, arms eager to offer what I've asked you to give. Come knowing that your great joy is My desire. Come believing that I want to give you more than you could ask for or even imagine. Come trusting that I will complete what I have begun in you—and that all that you are and all that you will be is part of My story in you."

I want you to remember this whether your life looks like a continual story line or a series of chapters. I want you to remember this when opportunities are presented like gifts and when disruptions cause the ground beneath you to quake. God is a masterful designer of your "and in itself and."

PART 4

RECLAIMING YOUR STRENGTH

PBS aired a documentary called *Half the Sky* that showed women around the world in patriarchal societies doing incredible things like working on infant mortality. Here I am in the US, and I have zero excuse not to do what's in my heart. It took five years for me to form the Root Collective. Now we work with multiple businesses in Guatemala to source our products. We focused on our shoes for a while, and now we're branching out into other goods. I can't change the world, but I realized something else: the artisans living in these communities, the people whose poverty I wanted to change . . . we can fix it together. That change can come from partnership.

from an interview with Bethany Tran,
president, the Root Collective

Many women have done wonderful things,
but you've outclassed them all!

Proverbs 31:29

12

Monja Blanca and Acatenango

If you look on the back of the Guatemalan fifty-cent piece, you'll find a flower. It represents beauty, art, and peace. Its name is Monja Blanca, "White Nun," a rare orchid so named because it looks like a holy woman kneeling in prayer, the brilliant white blooms contrasting with the purple flowers of the orchids around it. I love the story so much that I collect the coins every time I visit the country just so I'll have them to share the story of Monja Blanca's glorious truth.

I picture the Monja Blanca as a woman with nearly everything she needs to grow and bloom on her own. She needs no pollination to blossom. In fact, the Monja Blanca lacks only one thing to thrive. She needs support to stand. A fence post or tree trunk provides just the strength she needs to rise. Now, if you were to go to Guatemala to find the Monja Blanca, you might have to wait a while. It takes her fifteen years to bloom, and then her flowers last for only a short season.

Also in Guatemala, you'll find a landscape dotted with volcanoes. Many are active, and the puffs of smoke that rise each day are reminders of the power that lives beneath the peaks. The most active of these volcanoes, Fuego, spews smoke and ash daily, and its lava flows are a constant threat. I've seen the sky light up with fire and felt the earth quake with Fuego's anger. In fact, in 2018, Fuego erupted with such force that pyroclastic flow took out an entire village within seconds. Scientists say the people in that village likely never knew what happened, as the white-hot liquid and volcanic rock moved at speeds of up to seven hundred miles per hour.

Fuego seems hell-bent on destruction.

But standing next to Fuego is its sister, Acatenango. Yes, I also see Acatenango as a woman. She's a quiet giant as she faces the fury of her smaller, disgruntled twin. Acatenango is best known as host to hiking expeditions structured around watching Fuego. But she is also famous for her coffee. Some of the most flavorful beans in Guatemala are found on her plantations—plantations that are enriched by the volcanic ash of her twin. Fuego's fire gives birth to Acatenango's strength.

■ ■ ■ ■

You might wonder why I'd liken a lily and a volcanic mountain to women. It's because of Tia Lilly and Lucy, two powerful souls living on opposite sides of the world. To me, Tia Lilly is like the Monja Blanca. And she is raising up orchids all around her. You'll find her on a Guatemalan hilltop at Hope & Future, a home for young women who have been sexually exploited.

And I see the beautiful redemptive story of Acatenango in Lucy, a former nun who now cares for children and families living with HIV in northeast India.

Like Tia Lilly and Lucy, I believe you are like the Monja Blanca. And the redemptive strength of Acatenango lives in you too.

The orchid blooms in its season. The coffee that tastes the best is born from the worst of circumstances. Strength is revealed in weakness. Things take time, and time takes its toll, and yet we rise. Culture may tell us there are limits to our usefulness and that disruptions and delays are the enemies to our success, but trust me on this: there is no "too soon" or "too late" or "too long" or "too lacking" in you. God's strength is found in you right now.

13

Tia Lilly and Lucy

The girls and I sat under the shade of a tree that had kept watch over the hill long before there was a home or a playhouse or a garden. The youngest was only twelve. She had been held hostage for two years as a slave until one of her captors looked away long enough for her to escape and run to the authorities. Now, five months pregnant, the young girl was learning about self-worth and redemption.

We talked about our dreams and our fears. And we talked about Tia Lilly, the woman who had invited them all into a place called Hope & Future and who now carried in her name a title of familial affection—Tia or Aunt.

"If Tia Lilly was sitting in this circle, what would you say to her right now?" I asked.

"I would tell her thank you for saving my life."

"I would tell her I love how she speaks to me. She makes me feel special."

"This place—the name of this place is my favorite because it is true. Here I have hope. And here I have a future."

I looked around at all the girls, tears welling up in my eyes because of the truths they spoke. "And how many of you want to be like Tia Lilly when you grow up and help make others feel valued and important?"

Without hesitation, everyone raised their hands. The girls. The visitors from the US. And me.

There is something about Tia Lilly. You feel divine strength when you meet her. Though she's been the director of Hope & Future for less than a decade, her belief in rising above the pain has been strong in her since she was two.

That's when her father abandoned her.

"My father was a troubled man. He was unable to be faithful," Tia Lilly shared as we sat near a picture window overlooking the Guatemalan countryside. "I have twenty-three half siblings. *Twenty-three*. I have met maybe five of his lovers. I don't know why he could never be happy. But he always had problems—even on his wedding day. He left my mother at their reception, and he didn't return for one week."

She remembers the day he left them for good. "My mother was so afraid. I was the youngest of four, and I was the only girl. To make money to care for us, she opened a little restaurant. She would cook all day Saturday, and then we would all try to sell the food on Sunday. We would hold back a little bit of food for us to eat, and we would use any money we made to pay bills. But there were so many days when we had nothing."

When Tia Lilly was seven, her mother left for the United States, taking a job as a housekeeper in a home near New York City's Central Park. Lilly and her brothers were left with a caregiver, but it was Tia Lilly who took care of the house. "My brothers were so much older and were rarely at home. I would make a soup of broth and put spices in it to eat. Sometimes it would be too hot or taste so bad. But I would try. And I would wash the clothes and clean the floors—things I had seen my mama do. I had one pair of shoes that I glued together time and time again. I felt so alone and afraid."

Her mother returned for her children three years later after receiving permanent residency in the United States. Tia Lilly remembers her mother walking each day from Hell's Kitchen to Fifth

Avenue to save cab fare. "We lived in a tiny one-room studio in a nondescript apartment building originally constructed for Irish immigrants. The bathtub was in the kitchen, and there was no privacy at all. My mother made forty dollars a week, and half of her earnings went to the rental of the apartment. My brothers were with us only a short while before moving to New Jersey, where they could earn five dollars an hour doing construction work. So again, I was left alone—this time in a huge city. The threat of abuse was all around me. I was able to protect myself, but it left a deep impression—one I still remember when I work with the teenage girls here."

Tia Lilly had a passion to learn, and she received a fellowship to a special program at the Rockefeller Center, where she was mentored by successful businesswomen. When she closed her eyes, she could see herself as one of them. She and her mother stayed in the Hell's Kitchen apartment until Tia Lilly was in high school. Then they moved to Brooklyn, where she continued to thrive.

Tia Lilly was an excellent student, and she just knew she would be accepted to Columbia or NYU, where she would study to become a nurse or a psychiatrist. But opportunities were limited for students in the public school system in New York, and she instead found herself at a local community college.

Then a two-week holiday vacation to her homeland of Guatemala changed everything.

To Help Make Their Lives Whole

"After my freshman year, I wanted to take a bit of time to just relax. I wasn't expecting to fall in love with the country of my childhood. I begged my mother to allow me to stay for a year." Tia Lilly immersed herself in studies and became an administrative assistant. She also met and married her husband, an attorney. He encouraged her to follow her dreams, and she joined the staff of a local orphanage. She worked with teenagers every morning and did administrative work in the afternoons. "I hated the smell of the orphanage. It didn't smell like home at all. And I can still close my eyes and feel the touch of one of the little girls there. She would come and stroke my arm just to know someone was there. She was so hungry for love."

The harsh environment of the institution was unlike what her mother had described. She, too, had been an orphan and for years had found safety and belonging in a small Christian group home. "I knew then I wanted to have a home like that, a family environment where I would teach orphans everything I could to help make their lives whole."

Tia Lilly typed up her vision and tucked the pieces of paper away for safekeeping. She continued to teach at the orphanage while she furthered her own education. Soon she was transferred to a school in Guatemala City where she taught children with special needs. As she invested in her students, she learned their stories, discovering that all had come from broken homes and hard places. She longed to do something more for them, but doors remained closed to her dream of opening an orphanage. Instead, she grew more successful as an educator and soon became the vice principal of a prestigious English school in Guatemala City.

"And then I got sick. Very sick. Even with emergency care in a major city, I was unable to work. Illness took a year from me," Tia Lilly said. "If it wasn't for that sickness, I wouldn't be here right now. Hope & Future wouldn't be here."

While she was sick, a cousin invited her to listen to a woman who was visiting from the United States—a pastor who was speaking at a local church. Tia Lilly had no desire to attend, and she was in severe pain the day of the event. But she listened to the woman's testimony, and everything changed.

"I fell in love with Jesus at the age of thirty-six. I was healed that night. It was like a curtain opened up and I could see it all—my father's brokenness, my mother's pain, my own failings, all the blessings I had received, why I was in Guatemala, why I had been given the gift of my husband, why my mother had shared all her stories of the orphanage, and why I had written those pages years before. It was all clear. Everything came together."

Tia Lilly returned to work with a newfound passion and commitment. Like the Monja Blanca, she had been given the strength to stand. She knew her purpose, and she believed God would open doors in time.

Each One Belonged to Someone

The first door would be to a baby home in San Lucas. There Tia Lilly cared for discarded little ones from newborn to three years of age.

In 2012, Tia Lilly was called to rescue a little boy named Diego. He had been found in a septic tank, injured and very sick because of the waste he had been inhaling. When she arrived to receive him, she was asked if she could take two more infants. One, a little girl named Dulce, had been found in a hotel, wrapped in toilet paper and placed in a trash can. The other, a little boy named Armando, had been found outside in a sack covered with leaves and rocks. "It was only his loud crying that alerted police to his whereabouts. There was no way I could say no to caring for the infants."

As she and a volunteer drove away, she looked down at the babies. "Diego was on my lap on a pillow to protect his fragile body. Dulce was cradled in my right arm, and Armando was snuggled in my left. I realized that all three had come from the same circumstances. I realized that each one of these children belonged to someone—someone who was afraid and desperate. God placed a drop of hope in me that something could be done." She began weeping. "At that moment, I felt so very small and helpless to do anything. My friend looked back at me holding the babies and crying. 'You can do this, Tia Lilly. God will give you strength to do this.'"

Holding those little ones, Tia Lilly felt a longing rise up within her, a conviction wrapped in strength and confidence to dive deeper into the issue of teen pregnancy. Hope & Future was born. The teen moms came, each with her own story of abuse. Tia Lilly offered respite to these young mothers and their little ones. The strength she had embraced in her own life became the strength she poured into theirs.

Everything Has Meaning

While Tia Lilly is like the Monja Blanca, Lucy is most certainly Acatenango.

"I think I'd like to marry one day, but I don't know if I could find someone to keep up with me." Lucy looked at me and laughed as she imagined what it would be like to share her journey—this adventure that's looked so different from the one she and her family dreamt she would live.

I've told you some beautiful stories about Guatemala. But one of my favorite places to be in this world is Aizawl, the capital of the state of Mizoram in northeast India. There the clouds nestle easily into valleys, and the gray of the skies brightens the thick green jungle that surrounds Gan Sabra, a quiet sanctuary for children of all ages living with HIV. Chickens cluck quietly outside in a handmade coop made of tin and wood. Lucy, who founded the home and works there daily, loves to open the windows of the home to take it all in—the rain and children's laughter and dogs barking and those chickens.

I once asked Lucy what her favorite room in the house is. In the secluded sanctuary of Gan Sabra, I love the prayer room on the second floor where the kids sing praises at the top of their lungs and cover my tear-stained face with their hands as they ask God for blessings on the aunty from the US who dances with them.

When I asked, Lucy responded with a smile. "I've never thought about what my favorite room in the house is. Any room with the kids is my favorite room."

She wrapped a piece of betel nut in a leaf carefully spread with raw lime. My friend Uma says chewing betel is Mizoram's only bad habit, and it seems to be something done by everyone there. The habit stains Lucy's lips the same blood-orange carnelian color as the precious stones hand chiseled to adorn the Taj Mahal, one of the world's greatest wonders that stands in majesty thousands of miles away in mainland India.

Lucy is like a precious stone, and she is far more beautiful than the Taj. Her phone rings constantly. A school calls or a mother is in crisis or a social worker has the story of a child found chained. With each fiery storm, Lucy grows stronger.

On that rainy afternoon as we sat talking, she paused for a moment and stared into my eyes. "Everything has meaning for you. I saw it in your eyes when I first met you. We are alike in that way."

Lucy's childhood wasn't at all like those of the children she now cares for at Gan Sabra. Growing up in northeast India, she had a very normal, very simple childhood. A quiet Catholic girl, she lived in a peaceful home with loving parents until she finished seventh grade. "The good schools were far away, so I was placed in a hostel at a convent to complete my education. I was there until I was fifteen—until tenth grade."

Lucy was then faced with a life-changing decision. "The nuns at the convent wanted me to join them. They were so persistent. They would ask me and then ask my family if I was interested. Honestly, I really hated the idea of being a nun. They scared me. I hid from them. I didn't understand them—how anyone could give so much of their life to God. But one day I was in church, and it hit me that I had to face the thing I feared. So that day I said, 'Here I am.' My parents were surprised. I was surprised. But I felt God was calling me."

She left that day and joined the convent. For thirteen years, Lucy studied and prayed and served faithfully. She thought she knew what it meant to fully trust God, and her faith in Him was strong. Her brother and sister also joined the ministry as a priest and a nun. For Lucy, life was beautiful and purposeful. She believed she would be a nun forever.

That is, until 2004.

Like a Love Letter

"As nuns, we made our vows to God every year. But that year it was time for me to make my vow permanent. I was ready to do it, but I felt a need to take time to pray and fast. So I asked to go on a retreat, where I fasted for forty days and nights, seeking God in front of the blessed sacrament. I spent time with Jesus.

"Before I went on the retreat, I never thought about leaving. Even with the challenges there—because we are human even in convents—nothing made me want to leave. But after thirty days of fasting, I was sitting in front of the blessed sacrament, and I felt Jesus tell me it was time to leave. I still remember my response. 'Come on, Jesus, what will people say? What will I do? Nuns don't just leave. What reason do I have?'

"But I continued to hear His voice: 'Just come.' I have never forgotten that day, when I just knew that no matter what, He was with me. I poured out all my fears to Him and left them in His hands."

After the forty days, Lucy delivered a tear-stained application to leave the convent. Though it was difficult to write, Lucy poured out her heart onto the page. Under "reason for leaving," she struggled. There was no hurt. She wasn't unhappy. It would have been so much easier had there been a reason. But there was no reason other than "because."

For a while, Lucy wore her habit—the only clothing she had known for thirteen years. It was like a bridal gown to her. "I had taken a vow of poverty, chastity, and obedience to Jesus. It was my life, my wedding day. When you take your vows to become a nun, you get to select the songs and Scriptures that are most meaningful to you, and they're used at your ceremony. You also write a prayer—your personal vows to Jesus. I was leaving the convent, but I wasn't leaving those vows.

"On October 14, 2004, I attended my last mass as a nun. Only one sister knew I was leaving. I hadn't shared my heart or my plans with anyone else. That morning the songs sung and the Scriptures read were the same as those of my special wedding day. Have you ever heard the song 'Not My Own but Saved by Jesus'?[1] You should listen to it sometime."

For a moment, her story paused, and she was at that mass again, swept up in the nineteenth-century hymn that is still her anthem.

Lucy had written a prayer when she joined the convent, and at that final mass, after receiving the sacrament of communion, she wrote new words: "Lord, to Thee I make my commitment to You again. Thy will be done in and through me. Let me feel Your presence close to me. Let me be filled with Your love. Lord, I need You and only You. Oh, Lord, I once again bring all that I am and all that I long for. Thine for all eternity."

She signed it like a love letter.

With no firm plans in place, Lucy stayed with her parents for a while and tried a few odd jobs to see if anything felt right. She even thought about being a teacher but missed the only train that could take her to school in time for the classes. Then the sisters from the convent asked her if she would be interested in volunteering at a local addiction shelter during the Christmas holidays. Soon Lucy was on staff at the shelter as a caseworker for those who found refuge there.

When a prostitute came into the shelter ready to give birth after several failed abortion attempts, Lucy came face-to-face with the reality of HIV. The woman gave birth to a baby girl and then abandoned her after only a few days. Lucy tried to find a home for the child, asking family after family to take her in, but the stigma of HIV was too strong and the fear too great, and all refused.

"I asked my parents what they would think of me—a single woman—raising a child with HIV, and they said they believed I could do it with God's help. So I prayed, and I knew God's answer was yes to my being a mother. I also knew it meant I would no longer work at the shelter. It was no place to raise a child, and I had to focus my attention on her. I had no other work, but I had God's provision."

Lucy named her daughter Jessica and cared for her as best she could. Word quickly spread that she was raising a child who was HIV positive, and social workers called her to ask if she would consider adopting more. Throughout the state, children were being found locked away or tossed aside because they were born infected with an illness considered a death sentence to all who came in contact with it.

"You never *see* the hands of God. You just move to them. I knew nothing about HIV or anything. But it was because of the sisters in my convent that I met the child who would change my life." Lucy opened a home for children living with HIV and named it Gan Sabra, which means "flower in the desert" in Hebrew.

In the midst of the fire of oppression against children with HIV, Gan Sabra blossomed.

14

Refined, Not Defined

I wish I could say I've easily embraced the idea of being like a Monja Blanca or an Acatenango. Tia Lilly and Lucy have been generous role models for a woman who is far more a maelstrom of self-fulfilling prophecy, of "If it's gonna get done, I guess I'm just going to have to do it *now*" wrapped up in tight bands of "What does it matter—I'm too old to even try." Of all the things I've learned, this might be the lesson that's taken the longest to find its home in my heart. I say with bravado that I will wait on the Lord's timing and rest in His strength, only to be easily shaken by days that sometimes feel like foreboding fortresses or crazy fun house slides. I pray to be a woman who is *refined* rather than *defined* by circumstances. I want to become more honorable through hardship, but I catch myself playing the victim when time isn't cooperative or gentle or encouraging. There are moments I'm far less like Tia Lilly and Lucy and far more like Sarai and Hagar.

At the age of seventy, Sarai had been given a promise from God that she would become a mother. She wanted to believe, wanted to have faith, wanted to hold a child in her arms. She wanted it so badly, in fact, that she devised a plan to fulfill that promise.

Hagar was her servant. She likely wanted to please Sarai, wanted to be seen as worthy and capable. She wouldn't have known that being a servant would include becoming pregnant with her master's child. But as her owner, Sarai used her power to ensure the promise she was given came true—even if it meant forcing an Egyptian slave to sleep with her husband.

Though their circumstances were different, both women shared the same doubt—that God would actually be strong enough to uphold His promise.

I don't know about you, but I have been Sarai. And I have been Hagar. I've struggled to believe that I'm not the strange exception to God's promises. I have doubted God at His word. I've been willing to take matters into my own hands and compromise what I know to be true, just to make things happen. And I have felt helpless to stand up to the compromise of others. I have been the abuser of promises made. And I have been the abused.

Sarai and Hagar both learned that God was indeed faithful. Sarai became a mom years later—and became Sarah, mother of the nations. Hagar was the first woman in Scripture to be personally blessed by God. They both questioned Him, and yet He remained faithful. I've questioned so much, *and yet* God shows Himself trustworthy to keep His promises. God is faithful to keep working His powerful, hopeful, grace-full love in and through my life. He holds out His strength and says, "This is yours."

Both Tia Lilly and Lucy have taught me that God is in the thick of it all with me. He is there to wrap around and hold our days, ready to remind us of His power and His tender kindness. He's there to show us the twinkle in His eye as He walks with us and watches us tend to all we've been given. He is faithful even on the days we allow other things to get in the way of our fidelity. He is trustworthy even on the days we allow other things to catch our eye. He is present even on the days we are overwhelmed by the past or the future. He is there even on the days we face the fortress or the fun house slide.

God is there to remind us that His timeline always trumps ours. In His chronology, there's no too young, too old, too lacking. In

His design, our design is perfected—no matter our geography, pedigree, address, heritage, big plans, or failed attempts. He is there to strengthen us so we may in turn strengthen others. He is there to take the fury that threatens and transform it into beauty and power.

15

God's Strength Is Yours

More Than a Home

Around twenty-five children and teens now call Hope & Future home. Tia Lilly carries the stories of countless young mothers in her heart and advocates relentlessly for their protection and freedom. Every girl at the home is a story of rescue and redemption. All have been abused physically and sexually, and most are moms.

I think about all the young women I've met in government orphanages around the world. Many who are victims of rape or incest struggle to find within themselves affection for an infant who is a constant reminder of their abuser. But at Hope & Future, the young mothers embrace their infants with such tender care. Watching them is a sign of just how powerful and deep God's restoration is in even the darkest of circumstances.

Hope & Future truly feels like a big family. Lilly attends to every small detail to make sure the home is a sanctuary for healing. All the kids assist with chores, and the young moms help one another with diaper changes, playtime, and cuddling fussy infants. Everyone receives regular counseling, and everyone participates in a customized academic program based on their specific needs.

Lilly knows from her own life how important education is for the children in her care. "I was a teacher for almost twenty years before having an orphanage. I see now that it was God's plan. They always assigned me the children who had challenges, those who came from hard home lives and traumatic situations. And I volunteered my time at hospitals to counsel those who were suffering. Almost every child at Hope & Future has learning difficulties because of the trauma they've experienced. They need to be given every opportunity to excel."

Lilly has taught me that beginnings may arrive at any point in our lives, that the plans we thought were firmly in place are in fact clay in the hands of a God who loves us enough to keep making us useful for service. She's taught me to keep my eyes open for the "next" and the "what-if" and the deeper stories tucked inside the pages we're living, like margins filled with notes to make those stories richer and more purposeful. She has taught me that the Lord points us in new directions even as we're moving in the one we believe to be true. She has taught me that there is no shame in saying, "But I am not equipped," because the Lord is the one who equips us as His Monja Blancas, and He delights in upholding us with His strength.

And she continues to show me that a woman with fire in her soul will find strength in her legs to keep walking. One afternoon as we watched the girls play outside, Tia Lilly said, "I still think about the day in that pickup truck, the day with those infants when I was so afraid because I was not young and not an expert and so unsure. God said that day, 'It will be hard, but don't worry.' It was always in His plan for Hope & Future to be here."

Each time I look into Lilly's eyes, I see wisdom and love—and I see God kindle new flames of hope within her. While others would be content with all that's been accomplished, she continues to dream. She sees more than a children's home on the hill. She sees a place where a community can be changed for the good. She's teaching accounting to the girls as they learn to grow and sell avocados to neighbors. She looks at the street below and dreams of a retail area where small businesses could be launched—a bakery, a vegetable stand, or maybe even a beauty shop. In the future, perhaps there could be a medical clinic and a place for job training for the entire neighborhood.

There's never a time when Lilly doesn't carry a notebook with her to catch the dreams. As she and I talked about the future she sees in her mind's eye, that same notebook caught her tears. "More than anything, I dream for every child who is part of our family here. I pray their hearts are healed so they will be opened even more to learning and growing. I want to see each of these children grow and be successful in whatever they chose to do with their lives. I dream that it will be Tia Lilly at each of their weddings as their mama. The older girls have shared with me that they want to marry Christian men. I share with them that those men are out there and that they are praying the very same thing—that they'll marry good-hearted Christian women. I dream about those days. What a celebration that will be."

Die for a Noble Cause

Lucy focuses on celebration too, though for her and the kids at Gan Sabra, those celebrations are found in daily milestones. "We have chickens and dogs so our kids will learn to love well," she shared as Marshall, one of those dogs, peeked in on us and then settled in for a nap. "Everyone does chores here—we all do our share. We are called to work until we stop breathing. Our only rest is in Jesus."

She stepped away for a moment to encourage the children as they worshiped in the prayer room upstairs and then rested again next to the open window.

"You know what my greatest wish is? My wish is that even if I die, I want to die for a cause. I don't want to just die peacefully. We think that's a blessing, right? To go peacefully in our sleep. I don't blame those who believe that. But as for me, I don't want to die that way—that's a soft way. My life is so short, and I will die once. So I want to die for a purpose, for a noble cause. Sometimes the kids die in our home, and it's hard to deal with. But God is giving us strength. Only when you trust Him do you see miracles. Expenditure will always be greater than income. But His miracles are always greater than both. Miracles happen. We always have enough.

"You know, I used to think, *These kids are lucky to have us. Through Christ, we are providing their lives with meaning.* But now I know it's just the opposite. Because of them, I have been given meaning. When I give my life away to others, my life is meaningful. I thought the only way to have meaning was to do one thing. Now I know different. God's ways are higher. He is not lacking in plans for us."

Lucy's heart is carrying on in the hearts of the children. Not one sees their life as lacking. Every child at Gan Sabra wants to pour out their life for others when they grow up. Knowing abuse and neglect, they now want to be doctors and teachers and social workers who care for those who can't care for themselves.

There's Allen, raised by a leper woman in the jungle after his family abandoned him, who wants to be a doctor so he can care for the truly poor. And Tanya, once locked in a hut for years and fed through a slot in the door, who believes she is called to teach and shatter the myths about HIV in her state and in her country. And Nelly, a precious teenager who was raped by the very family members who infected her with HIV, who believes her calling is to help others learn to forgive.

Lucy smiles because she knows that God's story within everything is greater and that He can be trusted with each switchback and hairpin turn, every deep and shadowed valley, and every mountain-peak moment that takes our breath away. She has taught me that in the same way His will is expansive, His story in and through us is bigger than any of our chapters and that in Him there is always the chance to begin again and again as He turns the pages. Though the fury and the fire threaten, He remains faithful. There is no end to the story, no real false start, no walking a road only to have to walk back and start over again. No, the stories found in us are stories unfolding, with fresh strength given time and time again.

"There are those who believe that moving from one thing to another is wrong—that God wants us to have stability," Lucy shared on that rainy day as we listened to the children play and watched Marshall sleep peacefully. "There are those who will take a step and then stop to rest in the security. And there is a place for those people. But the truth is, God has few people He can truly send, few people who will pick up and move as He wills. I used to worry, 'What will they say of me—a nun and then a teacher and then a caseworker and now a director of an HIV home? They will say, "That Lucy, she does not know what it is she is to do."' But I am following God. And He is looking for others who aren't afraid to follow, no matter the cost to our security or stability."

She then looked at me. "You are one of those people. I saw it in your eyes when I first met you. We are alike in that way. And there are others."

Lucy said God is looking for people who are unafraid to move because He has so much to share.

She's speaking to you, friend. You've reclaimed your design, purpose, and shape. Now it's time to reclaim your strength.

In Him, you are like the Monja Blanca. You are Acatenango.

PART 5

RECLAIMING YOUR WORTH

The art started out as a self-care thing. I was struggling with anxiety at the time. Six months prior, I'd been diagnosed with bipolar disorder. My mind was way too loud, and I needed something I could do with my hands. My work isn't the clean, popular, Instagram kind of work. But do I want to make art that is weird and provocative and challenges people? That triggers memories, helps them process something, or gives them ideas? Or do I just want to make and sell art that is pretty? The color is in me, and it's what I have to offer. That creative sense, it's in us. It's just part of who we are.

from an interview with A'Driane Nieves,
founder, Tessera Arts Collective

She keeps an eye on everyone in her household,
and keeps them all busy and productive.

Proverbs 31:27

16

Disqualified

If we were sitting on the sofa getting to know each other right now, one of the things I'd say is, "Tell me about you—the real story of you." I don't know about you, but for years four words were embossed on my heart—words that affected my ability to serve others fully and lead gracefully.

Those four words were, "If you only knew."

While we lounged, I would ask you about the story of you, and then I would ask if it was okay for me to be candid with you about my story too. Yes, this book is about what I've learned from several women. But this particular story is a bit more personal—because it's given me permission to face the dark fear that threatens to paralyze us: disqualification.

The sense of disqualification we as women can feel because of age or appearance or education or birthplace can certainly try to hold us captive. But the sense of disqualification we feel because of our life stories? It hisses at us, "Certainly, nothing good could come from this."

■ ■ ■ ■

I took care to sit just so in my tailored business suit so I wouldn't wrinkle the paper on the examination table at the doctor's office—

a doctor's office that smelled far too much like appointments with my mom before cancer had its way with her only a year before. I remember thinking that day, *I'm not sick.* It seems unfair to make them have to clean this room.

The doctor walked in. A friend from church, he was a tender man with a soulful smile who only a few years before had diagnosed our son with an illness that, until that time, had been a head-scratching mystery. God had used this friend's wisdom and his bedside manner to bring healing to my precious son, and I was forever indebted. Now it was my turn to ask about the overwhelming ache that seemed to defy explanation.

"I think maybe something's wrong. With me," I said as he sat on the stool by the table and looked at my chart. "I mean, maybe there's nothing wrong. I don't know."

He looked at me. "So what's going on? Your blood pressure's great. Pulse is a little high, but that's not uncommon."

"I'm fine. Really," I replied as I felt my body stiffen into an authoritative pose.

Why do I do that? I thought. *I'm here because I'm worried—so why do I have to act like things are okay?*

I tried to relax my shoulders. "Things are going well. They really are. My job is great. Brad's job is great. I travel a lot—Brad and I both do—but it's all we've ever known, so it's fine. Ian is doing so well now—thank you. He's so healthy. Did you know he put on twenty-five pounds in one year thanks to your help? He's been accepted to Texas A&M. You know, 'Gig 'em Aggies!' and all. That's how you say the cheer, right? That's where you went?"

"Yep, that's where I went." He smiled, trying to keep up with the crazed speed of my voice. "He'll love it. You'll love it too."

I looked at him again. "I really don't know why I'm here. I guess—well, I just don't feel so great on the inside. My gut—it hurts a lot. I went to a dietitian once, and she tested me for food sensitivities. Lactose intolerant. Who would have known, right?"

I laughed nervously and then exhaled. "I thought it might be that again. I don't drink milk. Do you think it's my diet again?"

He grabbed my hand and said, "Calm down." I rolled my eyes at his statement. I was always in control. I didn't need his platitude.

"So what's going on?" he asked. "What do you feel?"

I paused, wanting my words to be perfect. It was so important to say just the right words. I was a business executive known for always having the right words.

"There are moments I find it hard to breathe—not like I can't catch my breath but like I can't slow down enough to remember to take one."

I laughed. He didn't.

"You know how it is, right? There are times I can't shut my brain off. There are times the insomnia comes, and it stays for days like an unwelcome guest. I've learned to just work when it happens—no need to waste good time awake, even if it's in the middle of the night. Sometimes my heart skips a beat or two. It feels like it's falling over in my chest.

"I don't drink much. I promise. My dad was an alcoholic, and the idea of getting drunk terrifies me, so I don't drink much, in case you were wondering. I don't. He fought so many demons, and he couldn't handle stress. My mom—did you ever meet my mom? She's the one who struggled—she battled depression. You know, I'm not like that. I don't even have high blood pressure. I'm healthy. Right? I'm really healthy, honestly." My eyes filled with tears. "But something . . . is different in me, something that makes everything ache and feel unwound. I don't know what it is."

The doctor grabbed a Kleenex for me and then said, "If you don't mind, I'm going to ask you some questions."

We talked about how I felt in the mornings and at night, how I responded to crises and to calm, where my emotions landed before and after simple things like eating. He asked what my goals were, what was important to me, and how I treated myself when I didn't meet a deadline. He asked pages of questions, and none had to do with my diet and the ache in my gut. Every piece of the conversation was about how I felt on the inside—if my insides conflicted with my outsides.

And when all was said and done, I received a diagnosis—one I didn't fully understand or want to understand. He called it generalized anxiety disorder. He could have called it anything, I suppose, because all I heard was, "You must be crazy."

And to me, crazy meant disqualified. Certainly, words like *anxiety* or *disorder* would disqualify me as a leader. A person who struggled with thoughts and feelings would most definitely be disqualified as a wife and mom and friend—as a Christian. Mental and emotional health are good qualifications only if the doctor's records read, "She's got it all together." But I didn't.

And yet God never labeled me crazy. In fact, He doesn't label any of us based on a doctor's records.

■ ■ ■ ■

I'm thankful for the dialogue about mental health that's growing in strength these days. When Jamie Tworkowski, founder of To Write Love on Her Arms, first shared images on Instagram of the pills in his palm that helped bring clarity to his days, I cheered. Now there are others who are doing all they can to help us see our brains in the same way we see any other organ in our bodies. Mental health is not unlike physical health, and caring for our brains in the same way we care for our hearts or lungs or kidneys should be accepted and encouraged.

But understanding mental health and receiving a diagnosis regarding our own mental health can feel a million miles apart. Understanding the connection between physical health, mental health, and our life stories can be overwhelming. And in an age when personal information is readily splashed across news feeds with little context as to whether what's to come is a refreshing rain shower or a devastating tsunami, we can find ourselves terrified that who we really are will be discovered—and we'll be disqualified.

After I received my diagnosis, I was given a prescription. The pills were highly successful in treating both anxiety and depression, and the dosage was low enough not to affect my performance at work. They did their job effectively. The pain in my gut subsided, regular sleep returned, and I didn't feel the constant rush of butterflies. No one at work knew about either the diagnosis or the treatment plan. It was only when I couldn't cry at my son's high school graduation that I realized something was still off. I could feel the emotion internally but couldn't express it at all. The treatment was doing a wonderful job of managing my anxiety, but it wasn't getting to the heart of why the anxiety was there in the first place.

You see, I was twenty-five when I sat in the passenger seat of a friend's Plymouth Arrow with my baby boy and all the pieces of our everyday life that small car could carry. That friend drove me toward an unknown future that would unfold and include college and a career, new cities and new friendships—and a decade of single parenthood. I had been taught to bootstrap—to be fierce. Though the concept of trauma was vaguely familiar, in my mind, it was something that happened to other people. I added "flee and begin again" to the list of hardships I would certainly overcome, and I kept moving. It was only after the failed treatment plan that I realized I couldn't simply press on. I needed to press in and make time and space for my soul to find healing.

Quietly, I looked for other ways to soften the emotional scar tissue that had never been provided the care it needed. I made a point to begin my mornings with prayer and Scripture reading, did my best to exercise regularly, and tried to get good sleep. My husband and I decided to move from the fast pace of a large city to a pristine lakeside community. I left the corporate world to work in full-time ministry. Though people noticed a change in me, only those closest to me recognized its true impact. It took years before I said anything publicly about the diagnosis or spoke openly about the pain or the healing that had come slowly and without great fanfare. The fear of being disqualified, "if you only knew," remained strong.

For me, the "if you only knew" was wrapped up in mental and emotional health. For you, it might be "if you only knew about my past" or "if you only knew about my life now" or "if you only knew how unsure I feel about my ability."

And then I met Flo. Through her I learned that "if you only knew" is nothing to fear.

17

Strength to Keep Fighting

As a single mom in a new city, Flo was overwhelmed by everything that seemed to disqualify her. She looked around at the house she purchased with the small amount of money she had saved. The barbwire-tough neighborhood showed no signs of welcome or comforting well-manicured homes.

Instead, there was evidence of a dog-fighting ring one street over, and rumors swirled about crack houses and gang violence. Flo took a deep breath and smiled at her daughter. "Well, here we are," she said softly. "It's all we've got."

The first time I met with Flo we didn't talk about being disqualified. Instead, she taught me about cats. Scooping up a kitten tucked under a cocktail table in her tiny living room, Flo looked at me with soulful eyes that had surely seen a million stories. "We find kittens and we tame them, or else it doesn't turn out good. The kids help out. It's good for them. It teaches them to be soft. My kids are hard when they get here. What they've seen and what they've been through makes 'em that way. But the kittens make 'em soft."

Her home is a bit like the scene from heaven in the movie *What Dreams May Come*. It's the same house in the same neighborhood in the same tough part of town. But now the house is drenched in color so thick that it seeps into every available space. The color can't help but spill out as it dances into the gardens and into the play area near the broken upright piano sheltered by a graffitied amphitheater.

Flo herself is a kaleidoscope, with ever-changing rainbow hair that never seems to want to stay in place. She loves Jesus and Bob Marley. Reggae is her worship music, and her hands are often stained from the paint used to decorate old guitars and statuary she then sells to raise money for the place she calls Comfort House.

"Did you see my African hut? It's next to the boat. I hauled the bamboo here myself. I know my kids may never get to go to Africa, so I wanted to bring it to them."

Everything about Flo's home—and her life—seems cobbled from dreams no one believed would come true. On paper, Flo would certainly be disqualified to dream at all. She grew up in a Chicago neighborhood not unlike the one that's become her home in Austin. It was there she found little love and little to eat and hard decision after hard decision. It was there that abuse haunted her nights. And it was there she tried to end her own life at the tender age of twelve.

"I took an entire bottle of aspirin. It was all I could find. I wanted to die, to leave the pain of my life. But God wouldn't let me. He wanted me to know I was worthy, that He had reason for me to be here. Something happened to me that day. I saw this light. It was Him, right with me."

Every time Flo shares the story of her thwarted suicide, she raises her hands in defiant joy. "Something happened, I tell you. I got strong. I came out fighting. God said, 'I've got work for you.' I didn't know what that meant, but I knew it was good."

It was a high school teacher who first noticed something different about Flo. "My homeroom teacher told me, 'You're going to amount to something.' I didn't have clothes that matched, didn't live in a decent neighborhood like so many of the kids who were in school with me. But I was friendly to everyone, and folks didn't seem to notice that I was so different. She saw that in me, I guess."

The teacher did indeed see something different about Flo—in the school cafeteria. At the beginning of the school year, tables were segregated by race—they had always been that way—until one fiery girl from the poor side of town decided to invite herself to a table so she could make a new student feel welcome. The teacher told her, "By the end of the year, everyone sat everywhere because *you* sat everywhere."

The teacher had seen something special in Flo's future. Mental health specialists didn't paint as bright an image. Instead, they labeled her with terms too large for a kid to carry. *Schizoaffective tendencies, manic episodes, possible bipolar disorder.* There were no trusted shoulders to help her carry the weight of her struggle. Instead, there were possibilities written on medical charts—shock treatment, institutionalization. But Flo remembered the light and the voice that told her she was worthy. And she remembered the words of the high school teacher who told her she would amount to something someday.

Those words gave her the strength to keep fighting.

Somehow Flo's fight landed her in Texas, in a neighborhood that felt like home to her past and salvation to her future. The little clapboard house was all she could afford in a city that she found welcomed broken people like her. Drug deals went down and women sold themselves to feed their families. And there was no place for kids to play.

It was the kids who gave her fight purpose.

18

Flo and Me

Flo's work started as a simple act of kindness. She would gather her pennies and purchase ice cream for the kids who had no place to play in the summer but the streets. She knew something needed to be done for them, and she knew they needed to hear God tell them they were worthy. She remembered how He had saved her life, and she wanted Him to save theirs.

Ice cream became a place to study when school started, and a place to study became a place to play when homework was done. Flo noticed teen moms who were struggling, and she knew their fear because she, too, had become a mom with little support. And she noticed the homeless who would find shelter in doorways on the busy streets near her home. A place to study and play became a place to get food when the cupboards were bare or to find diapers and formula when there was no money left. She fashioned a shower and dressing area outside for the ones afraid to enter in.

"Some people get freaked out when I open the house to homeless folks so they can get a meal and a shower. 'You're gonna get killed!' they say." Flo laughed and rolled her eyes, those arms raised again in celebration. "So what if I do? Maybe it's time for some rest. My bones ache. If God wants me home, let Him take me. But I'm still here, so I guess I'm still needed."

When her little yard became too small for the children who would visit, Flo prayed she would be allowed to purchase the vacant lot next door. But with no résumé and little money, she was ignored by realtors and lenders—that is, until Habitat for Humanity learned of her dream. They encouraged her to let people know about her prayer. "I had thirty-five cents in my pocket, and the lot cost twenty thousand dollars. In four days, twenty-four thousand dollars came in. You see how God is? He sees what stresses me.

"One time my house was on this tour of weird Austin homes. A stranger walked in and saw a statue I had decorated. His wife loved it, and he bought it—and the amount he offered was exactly what we needed to take care of some bills. God told me to do art. And it's art that helps. I was afraid to tell people my dream, but He sent someone to encourage me. Every time He meets needs. My friends from other parts of the world think everyone in the US is rich. They don't know our stories. There are months I'm not sure how we'll pay the bills. But there God is. He makes a way. Every time."

She's seen so much since she made the clapboard house her home—things that would harden the hearts of most people. But for Flo, the pain has only fueled her determination. "It's a Babylon world with hate and wars. If we can put rockets on the moon, why can't we put love in our hearts? God doesn't let us throw hate. We can't say we love Him and throw hate. The people I see who do horrible things? They are hurting. How can I hate people who are hurting?

"You know I take meds for bipolar. That scares some folks, so I don't talk about it much. But that's just who I am. I may battle good days and dark days, love, but I've only had madness in my heart one time. I had learned of a young girl who was being abused and trafficked, and I wanted to help her. What filled me with madness wasn't what was happening to her. She could be saved. It was her mother, who drove a nice car and lived in a nice neighborhood on the other side of town. She said she didn't have time to come get her. Love doesn't do that. Love shows up. The only way to fight the madness in me was to keep showing up."

So Much Color

Showing up day after day hasn't been easy for Flo. It's taken a toll on her physically and emotionally. For supporters, her eclectic artwork is a source of joy and a way to keep Comfort House funded. For Flo, working with her hands is healing. "I never did artwork as a kid. It was a gift God gave me to help me fight. Darkness tries to push in on all of us. It crowds in on me. That's why there's so much color here. I love color and brightness. Art helps push back the darkness so I can keep pushing back the darkness."

Scripture is filled with reminder after reminder that God delights in pushing back the darkness to reveal His purpose in our lives. I think about Hagar, a slave who was forced to bear the child of her master because his wife was determined to fulfill the promise God had made to her. It was Hagar who named God "the One who sees me," as He promised her a future still filled with hope (see Gen. 16:7–15). And there's Rahab, the prostitute woven into the very heritage of Jesus Christ. Working with young women rescued from sexual exploitation, I often wonder if Rahab was following in her mother's footsteps, or if she was sold into her trade, or if a friend told her, "Do what I do and you'll never be hungry again." Rahab was known for the bed she made available in a city that gave her space in its fringes and embraced her behavior as the norm.

So what was it about the spies that caused Rahab to clothe herself in newfound strength? I imagine them knocking on her door and asking for a place to sleep. They paid her but told her that her body was not what they wanted. They shared her time, her trust, her wisdom. They saw her as a woman. And Rahab felt seen. She felt known. She felt alive. And so she protected the men, believing in their words of freedom and hope beyond the battle that raged both around her and within her (Josh. 2:1–21). Rahab's life was redeemed as she became an ancestor of the Redeemer (Matt. 1:1–16).

I met Flo when she delivered a handmade beaded cross to my church and asked if we might have some volunteers who could help tend to her garden. Since then, Flo has taught me about cats and reggae music and how to make artwork from discarded things. But more than anything, Flo has taught me that nothing can disqualify us from God's purpose. There is no "if you only knew" piece of our stories that can't be redeemed for greater good. Because of her encouragement, I can now share my story without fear, knowing that God knows it fully and says, "I've got work for you."

Privilege and Pain

My story is one of visible privilege. I grew up in an upper-middle-class, predominantly white neighborhood, born to parents who remained married "until death do us part." As I was growing up, no one ever wondered where the next meal was coming from or if we were going to get to stay in our four-bedroom home next to a golf course. I was an exceptional student with a large circle of friends and three new cars before I turned eighteen.

But my story is one of hidden pain. Beginning again at twenty-five after a difficult marriage wasn't the first blow. My dad was an alcoholic, and his drunken rages often included threats against my mom and me. My parents remained married despite often saying they longed to be divorced. I was sexually abused by a close family member at the age of five—and instructed by my mom never to tell a soul because it could destroy our family's reputation.

But I wasn't just a victim of my circumstances. I was a willing participant.

I gave myself away far too young—and way too often. And I had an abortion at the age of eighteen. I actually made a list of pros and cons and decided my life trumped the life formed inside me.

By the age of twenty, I was weary of the external trappings and internal pain. I attempted suicide by overdose—and nothing happened. Nothing at all.

I wish I could say that, like Flo, I saw a light and heard God say, "I'm in this." Instead, I was angry that He had gotten in the way. It would take months before I would understand His salvation. It would take years before I would see His hand in my life.

And it would take Flo to teach me that there was not one part of that life that could disqualify me from fully living my God-given life.

Not even mental illness.

I am worthy of life because He has made me worthy.

19

You Are Holy Whole

I remember the day I gave Flo a clinging cross, a small wooden cross formed to fit perfectly in the center of her hand. "I know you deal with anxiety sometimes, Flo," I said. "I use one of these when I pray. It helps keep me focused. I battle with anxiety disorder, you know."

She put the cross in her housecoat pocket, smiling. "I'll keep it with me all the time." Then she turned and put her hands on my shoulders. "But listen to me now. A disorder is just a name. It's not the enemy, so there's no need to treat it like one. You have been designed by God to feel things differently. Your eyes have been created to see things differently. He's even got a purpose in that. Let Him show you."

Though medical experts may be wary about such advice, I have to admit that giving anxiety a little grace and love has calmed things down considerably for me. Sometimes it shows up because I'm trying to step too far into unknown futures and forgetting to tend well to the space that's been given to me now. Sometimes it rises because I'm simply not resting in what I know to be true. And sometimes it comes because I'm feeling the weight of someone else's pain. I'm learning to be quick to pray. That's definitely something not only Flo but also each of the other women I've mentioned do well. They pray. Boy, do they pray.

They all pray because they all believe God is a Redeemer. And of all the women, Flo has taught me to believe with all my heart that God redeems even the most ravaged landscapes in our journeys. He transforms them into vibrant gardens that give life to all who come near.

His promise of redemption is found in Joel 2:25, where the Lord says He will restore the years the locusts have eaten. In striking detail, He describes not one but four different types of insects.

For years, I wondered why God would choose the imagery of locusts rather than a natural disaster or pain inflicted deliberately by humans. And then I learned that in certain parts of the world, a swarm of locusts is far different from the image I had in my head—cicadas that fill the air with the song of hot summer days. Instead, locusts fill the skies like storm clouds. A swarm can be larger than two square miles in size and contain fifty million locusts. That swarm can eat more in one day than forty thousand people can eat in a year. And when those locusts die, their rotting bodies can foul land and water, causing sickness and disease for years to come. It's no wonder God used them as a metaphor to convey the strength of His promises.

God says He can redeem what was stripped away, chewed away, and destroyed completely. Put in real-life language, God can redeem time, relationships, dreams, hopes, and purpose. There is nothing in your life that nullifies His redemptive power, because He sees you as worthy, as holy and whole. Flo lives that.

First Thessalonians says that God calls us two things: holy and whole. There's not a diagnosis or a disability that can strike that description from you or from me. He has determined our worth, and He promises to make that worth known.

> May God himself, the God who makes everything holy and whole,
> make you holy and whole, put you together—spirit, soul, and

body—and keep you fit for the coming of our Master, Jesus Christ. The One who called you is completely dependable. If he said it, he'll do it! (5:23–24)

God is with us. All of us. Each of us. No matter where we are. No matter who we are. No matter the pain. No matter the joy. In the day of oppression. In the day of pain. In the day of the shadow of death. In the day of the celebration of life. He remains Immanuel—God with us—not "God once was . . ." or "God might one day . . . " He is *here*. Right now. Today. In this moment. In the midst. He is here with you and with me and with us.

I wish I fully understood why He doesn't keep us from pain. I wish I could fully comprehend why He doesn't simply fix everything quickly. I still have moments when I question and wonder. I have days of great faith and days of intense doubt. But even then He is Immanuel. Evil doesn't discount Him. Sin can't destroy Him. God continues to be with us. And in the midst of it all, He is restoring, redeeming, repairing, rebuilding. He is making all things new, starting with us.

So if we were sitting together on my couch, I would ask about your life. And if Flo were there, she would smile and tell you that every story has purpose—stories of provision and protection, stories of rescue and restoration, stories of doubt and fear and wonder. She would tell you that you are qualified. You are worthy because He is worthy.

PART 6

RECLAIMING YOUR VOICE

Someone asked me once who I'd love to invite to my house for dinner. I said Jesus—but it wasn't a cliché answer just because I'm a Christian. I would really love to see what He would do at the table. Would He sit down first and invite people over, or would He sit down last and serve everyone? What would He say, and who would He talk to? Would He be the one to introduce everyone, or would He be the one to listen to every conversation? I want Jesus to always be present at the table.

from an interview with Sarah Harmeyer, founder and chief
people gatherer, Neighbor's Table

When she speaks she has something worthwhile to say,
and she always says it kindly.

Proverbs 31:26

20

Language and Miss Mary

I sat with a Bible teacher one muggy morning outside a crowded Starbucks, listening to him reminisce about his days as a missionary who traveled the world to share the good news. He boasted about the size of the crowds everywhere he spoke and the throngs of desperate souls clamoring to get to the stage to profess their faith in Jesus.

"That's impressive," I said. "So then what happened?"

"What do you mean?" he responded, furrowing his brow. "That is our priority. We preach the gospel. There are thousands of people now going to heaven because of what happened in those countries."

"Oh, I get that," I said. "But what happened after you left? Who walked alongside them to care for them? It's great that they're headed to heaven, but who's helping them make it here on earth?"

He took a deep breath. "*That* is the reason we're meeting this morning," he said. He had written some books, and he wanted me to help him get them in the hands of more people. "These books need to be everywhere." He fidgeted in his seat, awaiting my recommendation on how to make it all happen.

"How wonderful that you've put so many books together," I said. "But I have to ask a question first. How do you know these books are right for *everyone*, regardless of culture? And do you have folks ready to translate them for you? *Everyone* encompasses a whole lot of languages."

He smirked. "Every word I share is from God. The Holy Spirit provides the understanding." He paused for a moment. "And everyone knows English is the language everyone wants to speak. I've got research that proves it. There's no need to translate. They'll come around."

I left the meeting, got into my car, and wept. "Sweet Jesus, what in the world?" I said out loud as I searched for a napkin in the glove box. "Why do we think it's on *everyone else* to understand *us*?"

> Speak up for the people who have no voice,
>   for the rights of all the down-and-outers.
> Speak out for justice!
>   Stand up for the poor and destitute! (Prov. 31:8–9)

The Beauty of Nuance

The first words out of Miss Mary's mouth were in Patois.

"Howdy mi people! Ow yuh uh duh do dis mawnin'?"

Patois is the language of most of the people living in Eden, the tucked-away neighborhood on a hill in Jamaica. Born of the demands of British colonists who forced West African slaves to speak English, the language is vibrant and melodic. The students Miss Mary taught at the Jamaican Christian School for the Deaf didn't know the familial power of Patois—but she did. It is the language she knew resonated with the families who viewed their deaf children as misfits, less than human, or demon possessed. And it was that language she used to fight for the rights of those children and to get them to the school that would provide a safe haven and a quality education.

Miss Mary spoke Patois fluently. She spoke English as well and effortlessly moved between the two, speaking to the staff of the school and then to the women from the US who had come to help build and paint cinder-block classrooms.

"I've gone to houses where children are enslaved and forced to do all the labor in the home because they are deaf," she quietly shared as she showed the team where they would be working. "They are treated as less than human, beaten, and ridiculed. And I won't stand for it. These children deserve a safe place to live; they deserve a loving place to live. They need an education, and they need good nutrition. You should see it when some of the children come to the school. They're terrified. They don't want to be held because all they've known is that hands are for beating. I am a hugger. I ache when someone doesn't want to be held.

"One student wept when it was time to go home, and I asked her what was wrong—because no child should cry about going to see their mother. I learned she had been abused by her stepfather, and she was viewed as an evil thing by her own mother because she was born from rape. She had become a slave in her home as punishment for being born."

The girl stayed at the school, and Miss Mary traveled to see the mother. "I told her, 'How dare you abuse your daughter! You should always look her in the face and tell her you love her. She is a nice, beautiful girl that God made. She didn't ask to be born as she was. But she is smart, and she has potential. And she deserves to be loved.'"

Miss Mary spoke not only Patois and English but also the language of the students. Her hands danced as she recounted Bible stories and called out kids who weren't paying attention. You could feel every nuance of every word.

In fact, it was Miss Mary who taught me that sign language is indeed that—a language. Every place I'd ever been employed in the United States made accommodations for the deaf community. Yes, "accommodations," things we hearing folks make to help those who aren't so lucky. The goal has always been to help those who were hearing impaired to be able to better understand us. Not once in my career did anyone suggest that I learn sign language. The task of communication was placed squarely on the shoulders of those who couldn't hear my southern accent.

The grace-filled power of language is rich in Miss Mary. She learned all the languages of Eden, and she used them to speak into people and culture and life.

They Can Hear

"Come with me, love," Miss Mary said as we walked through an opening in the fence by some classrooms and along a crude path leading to a bamboo grove. "I have something to show you." She smiled and slipped back into Patois. "*It wi mek yuh heart happy.*"

She praised God for the sunshine and for His mighty work as we first stepped into the shade of the bamboo. There was some statuary and a small bench waiting. "Sit, love. Close your eyes and feel. This is our prayer garden. I come here most days. The children come here."

The bamboo reeds creaked and moaned in the breeze. I expected to hear them. I didn't expect to *feel* their gentle dance. The ground vibrated softly beneath my feet.

Miss Mary whispered, "God speaks here. Everything that has breath praises the Lord. My children can hear the bamboo as it sings. They have no limits."

I fought back tears as we then walked to a pile of cinder blocks and sticks placed next to a large square of land that had been cleared. "This will one day be a church," she said, "a church where the students can worship in their own language. Can you just imagine? Oh, what a day that will be! Praise Jesus, what a glorious day!"

I wanted so badly to imagine what it would be like to *feel* worship in the vibration of a clap or a rhythmic march. I thought about all the times I had sat with church leaders around conference tables and dissected Sunday services I had helped produce—scrutinizing every song and lighting change, as if they held some sort of mystical power to impact a person's faith in God.

I prayed that my friends on this island wouldn't fall prey to the same fate, that they wouldn't define perfection as success and simple as shoddy. I prayed that those hands and unfiltered voices would become a testimony for every family in Eden. I felt that as long as Miss Mary was there to lead and help others learn to lead, everything would be okay, because she would speak the language.

21

What Others Need to Hear

What the Bible teacher said when we met was no different than the words of my mentors and teachers as I worked diligently on a career in broadcasting. "A southern accent doesn't bode well for a woman," my journalism professors said. "You need a General American dialect to be viewed as authoritative and credible." My voice and diction coaches were quick to point out each flaw in my pronunciation as I worked to hide my Oklahoma heritage by removing every colloquialism from my vocabulary and waking up any vowel that appeared lazy. Those professors and consultants were also quick to point out that pitch and inflection played into the power of a woman's voice. Emotional temperature must always be held in check.

I've mentioned some powerful stories about women from Scripture, but when it comes to speaking, there's no better example than Jesus. Jesus never took a voice and diction class, yet He knew how to speak the language of those who needed to hear what He had to say. He preached with authority; He taught with clarity. He spoke to the multitudes with the same attentiveness as when He spoke to friends at dinner. He became a farmer to those who tilled the land and a merchant to business leaders. He spoke courage to a woman terrified yet determined to reach out to Him for healing, and He spoke familiarity to a Samaritan stranger who longed to be known. He knew the language of slaves and of priests, and He was comfortable speaking to both.

What I was taught about the power of language to influence others and affect change was woefully incomplete. Jesus demonstrated that the true power of using our voices is found in speaking the language of those who need to hear.

I often wonder how Jesus would have crafted words on paper. He doodled a message in dirt that set an accused woman free and sent her accusers away, shaking their heads. No one knows exactly what He wrote that day. The Jesus words we know are all from His conversations—sometimes with a few folks, sometimes with a crowd. I don't think He sat with a pen in hand, looking for the perfect catchphrase to wow them or using heady language to elevate Himself. Instead, He spoke words that were accessible, memorable, and transformative. He spoke the language that others needed to hear.

I love that Scripture was written by many instead of one, that we experience poetry and prescriptive language, and that we get a firsthand look at the Godhead through the eyes of shepherds, kings, doctors, tax collectors, prophets, and priests. God's own creativity is revealed in the way His love letter to us is written. We witness His majesty and power, His tenderness and mercy, through a multitude of voices that all harmonize like a symphony. And God didn't stop there. He opened the door for theologians, historians, pastors, teachers, prayer warriors, and storytellers to dig deep and illuminate Scripture to speak to new generations. Eugene Peterson, pastor and author of the Message, says it took him twenty years to write the paraphrased Bible now used worldwide. "I spent a good five years learning the language of my congregation," he shared, "and that's what came out. I didn't think I was doing something that extraordinary, but I knew I was doing something for my congregation."[1]

I think God continues to demonstrate His love of language in every conversation that moves a heart toward mercy and grace, every story of faith and persistence, every prayer prayed. We need only to reclaim our God-designed voices. Miss Mary uses that God-designed voice well. And she's not the only one.

22

Lisa and Bianca

While Miss Mary uses Patois, English, and sign language to help those in need, Lisa speaks the language of empathy. She is fluent in grief and fear and anger. She reaches into her depths and pulls out emotions needed by those who are hurting. She feels the pain of the young women who are learning to be moms at the same age most are pondering prom dresses and future careers. Her conversations invite those teen moms into a safe space where healing can happen.

On Friday evenings, her quiet Grand Rapids, Michigan, home comes alive on a busy inner-city street. Kids play in the backyard, and teen moms take over the first floor. Volunteers from nearby churches serve food and cradle babies as the ministry called Grace's Table welcomes all without judgment. There's a good meal, gut-level conversation, prayer that isn't rushed, and always a family picture on the front porch. There used to be lots of room on the steps, but now they overflow with Lisa's family. They are all family to her.

Lisa didn't intend to give birth to a ministry. Then again, she didn't intend to give birth at seventeen either. But when a family comes unraveled, children so often do what they can to weave the frayed edges into something that feels like love. Lisa understands that pain and longing, and the tears can't help but fall when she talks about what breaks her heart for the young moms she loves.

"It gets to me when I hear people make comments to these young women like, 'You made an adult decision—so act like an adult.' They're not adults, and we need to care for them rightly. Or 'You've made your bed—now lie in it.' What a sentence to pass on to someone, to tell them, 'You're basically a screwup, and we're walking away so you need to figure it out.' What about the next twenty years of that mom and her child needing support and love and guidance? I understand the desire to have the girls rise up and be responsible. But I also know that unless the girls discover who they are in Christ and receive that love and that healing, they're going to continue to seek temporary comfort and temporary fulfillment."

Lisa is a weeper. I'm not sure we've ever had a conversation that didn't at some point include glistening eyes and a Kleenex or two. Happiness and heartbreak are equal recipients of the cleansing, healing, celebrating power of Lisa's tears. You feel this power as soon as they begin to fall—like oceans washing away the dirt and dross to reveal treasure.

Slow Miracles

A memory from her days as a single mom with a toddler was the culprit of the discontent Lisa was feeling one afternoon as we bundled up on a sofa and talked about the depth of her love for the young women. "I felt this pressing need back then. I knew there had to be other teen moms who needed support. The church can't just say, 'I'm glad she chose life.' Regardless of her decision, she needs support. I believe so strongly in walking with people, particularly through the mire. They don't need someone to solve their problems. They need people to be present. They shouldn't have to walk alone."

Our culture doesn't allow much room for slow miracles. Then again, neither did the culture in the days when Jesus invited folks to the table and visited homes. But He and Lisa are kin, unafraid to sit and listen and be present with a language that transcends words. Listening to her talk about Grace's Table, I find myself longing for more Friday nights in my life—safe places to be vulnerable and real and unafraid to be afraid. She wipes the tears away and laughs as she talks about how her life has changed as the girls have moved past uncomfortable pleasantries into stripped-down familiarity. None of it fazes Lisa.

"I always go back to hope, value, and purpose. If we can give them a flicker of hope that there is life for them right where they are, then we can work on value—knowing that they're loved, knowing that they're wanted, knowing that their presence is important and that life would be incomplete without them. Once hope and value are there, we can work on purpose—helping the girls to understand their unique role in this world, something they can give back to this world.

"And those three things don't happen overnight. There is no fast approach. It might take a lifetime for one person to establish that there's hope. In our world, we're so driven by measurable goals. I worked for years at a job where everything was based on metrics. In ministry, there is no metric for hope. It's hard to describe the progress the girls are making because a metric doesn't always work. I can't show you a graph for the change in a heart, but if you chose to invest six months of your time here at Grace's Table, you'd see it. It might not happen as quickly as you'd like it to, but you'd see the change in increments."

Lisa, like Jesus, knows the power of change that comes in fits and spurts rather than suddenly and with great fanfare. She lets her voice speak the language of love, a language that doesn't demand people understand but rather seeks to find the understanding within them.

More than the Words

One afternoon my friend Bianca stood in my kitchen, reading a chapter of a book by Chuck Colson. She was obliging me as I prepared to return to Romania, a country learning to breathe after almost being choked to death by communism. I had read the story in *Being the Body* before—the story of Laszlo Tokes, a pastor of the Hungarian Reformed Church who risked everything to bring back liberty during the days of torturous repression by Nicolae Ceausescu. But Bianca hadn't just read history books. Born in Romania, she had been raised learning to make Molotov cocktails and watching her parents worry if there would be heat in the winter or food for the family. She remembers the first time she tasted real bread. And she remembers when the communists set fire to her father's office building as a threat to those who longed for freedom.

I listened intently as she read the words from Colson's book aloud.

"A few blocks from this central square, on a corner across from a tram stop, sits a massive, ugly building. An optician occupies the ground floor on one side of the building; the other side is occupied by the Hungarian Reformed Church. On its gray stone wall two simple wreaths hang next to small plaques proclaiming in four languages: 'Here began the revolution that felled a dictator.'"[1]

I remember the first time I stood in that square in Timişoara, Romania. It was January, and the night sky was dripping with cold mist. A dead Christmas tree stood like a sentry in an upstairs window, and a cathedral glowed in the distance. I would visit again, when winter mist gave way to summer flowers. In all seasons, the bullet-riddled buildings hinted at the story that was deeper than history books.

Bianca continued, "'These were not only my parishioners, with a few Baptists and Adventists, but Orthodox priests and some of their Romanian flocks. I was very moved,' Tokes said, 'and it changes what I now see as my old prejudices—that we cannot make common cause, cannot fight side by side. Now that I have seen Romanians, Germans, Catholics, and Orthodox defending me, I know that I have to work for reconciliation between the nationalities and creeds in this country.' He called out in Hungarian and then in Romanian: 'We are one in Christ. We speak different languages, but we have the same Bible and the same God. We are one.'"[2]

I needed to hear Bianca's voice that day, because it told me far more than the words she was reading on paper. Her Romanian accent, her stops and starts, the frailty of her voice—they filled in every piece of the story and brought it to life. They gave meaning and substance. As soon as she opened her mouth, I was transported to a different place—a night illuminated by candles in an Eastern European village square, an army of everyday people standing with a pastor, resolute in the face of death as their country's heartbeat began again.

Her voice dropping to a whisper, Bianca looked at me and said, "This is truth."

It wasn't her words that moved me to tears that day. It was her dialect.

Bianca was trafficked as a young adult and sent to America, where she was matched with a partner. He was abusive. "When I decided to flee, someone gave me a women's Bible. It was my first Bible in English, and I poured over that thing. I'd never had need for it at such a deep level before, but it saved me. I was trafficked at a time when women who were trafficked had no rights. I was able to get out and start again, and that was a miracle. It was God's mercy. And if God's mercy was for me, then it's for every single person. I'm not the standard for that, but I'm a voice for it."

Bianca felt from the time she was a young girl that she wanted to help others, but she had no idea what that would look like in a world that offered few ways to care. But in the United States and on her own, she gained wisdom and knowledge. She eventually became a business consultant with a passion for helping small and emerging businesses with their core messages and value propositions. Bianca married again, this time to a wonderful man who supported her work and helped raise their two daughters. And the dream to help others continued within her. She invested time in women escaping abuse and neglect, helping them to rise and understand their value.

"Women have so many roles we're expected to play. In the last one hundred years, we've been taught that we aren't supposed to just be good at everything but *perfect*. And we set our standard not by ourselves but by other women. We compare not for the sake of comparing notes but to put ourselves down. That's the biggest problem I encounter. Shame kills us. There are more stories in the small little pools of life, the places where people get stuck, where so many women live in isolation in the messiness of living—and it's time we told those stories. The ways I see God working—in my own life and in the lives of these women—make me the life coach, the business coach, the minister, the mother, the wife. God is glorified in that as much as He is in any sensational tidal wave."

We are encouraged to work to find the right words in this world. We want to craft perfect sentences that will be remembered and revered—that will set people free and be oxygen to their souls. And we are demanding of others, that their words be just so, as if words alone have power to do anything. Words are indeed mighty things. Scripture passages speak about life and death being in the power of the tongue, and we wrestle the life-giving words into submission so we may harness them and use them like swords. We spend thousands of dollars on courses teaching unique for-mulas guaranteed to make our words work, how to adjust tone and inflection and pitch to make us sound more authoritative or persuasive. But the more I live this life, the more I see that it's not the actual words that have power.

The lives we live and the voices we have when we're not trying to find "the voice" give credence to whatever story we are trying to tell. The unique dialects in our voices reveal what we're made of; dialect points to our heritage—our bloodline. Our accents—their stops and starts, the emotions held within them—give our stories meaning and substance. And sometimes our stories need no words at all, because our dialects say all that needs to be said. I had been taught in college to discard my dialect. I learned from Bianca to embrace it.

Our dialects speak the truth about who we are and Whose we are. Our dialects tell others where we have been and where we long to be. If we have found life in Christ, His dialect resonates richly in us. Just listen. You'll hear it.

23

God Delights in Your Voice

When Miss Mary first tapped my shoulder on the porch outside the school dining room and challenged me to write a book, I thought she wanted me to share the story of the work being done at the Jamaican Christian School for the Deaf. She had a glorious dream of the island one day having a college—a school that would welcome the children she had grown to love and serve. I thought she wanted people to understand why she had sacrificed years with her own family to embrace the children of strangers and assumed she wanted the book to raise money to support her dream.

The last time I visited the school, Miss Mary shared the news of her retirement.

"*Laws, mi ave been here fi suh lang now,*" she said in Patois as she signed "weary" with her hands. She then smiled as she looked at the students gathering in the dining hall. Courtney and I had traveled to Montego Bay with our husbands to celebrate birthdays and anniversaries, and we had made the pilgrimage to Eden to see the woman who had become a friend and role model. The students had learned that it was my birthday. Miss Mary said they had a gift to share.

As they gathered, she quietly spoke. "You know, I was only staying a few weeks to prove to everyone that this wasn't where I was supposed to be. But then I started learning, and that learning kept me here. These kids have taught me about love and about being strong. I'm just sharing what they've been teaching me all along. That's all we're doing, love. We're just sharing what we've been learning. The good learning."

Miss Mary blinked back tears from her gleaming eyes and said, "I think it's time for me to learn from the girls now. They leave here, but they have nowhere to go. Their families don't want them, and they want to be loved, so they fall into the arms of men who hurt them. You remember Natalie, yes? She's in a bad way now." She wiped away more tears.

I closed my eyes and thought back to an afternoon under the shade of a huge breadfruit tree. It was my second visit to the school, and Miss Mary and I had found a bit of respite from the harsh sun to catch up on life. As we talked, I caught a glimpse of Natalie as she stepped out of her classroom. She smiled shyly, then walked over to the picnic table to join us.

Natalie snuggled in close to me, and we scrolled through the pictures on my phone until we found the one of us from our first time together—the one that had been taken what seemed like only a few days before. She leaned in nearer, and we took a new photo to celebrate our sweet reunion.

Slowly and carefully, Natalie spoke, "My mom had a baby." She then shared that she had three brothers and four sisters. None of them were with her at the school. They could hear, and they got to live at home.

As her sentences became longer, she grew weary of forming words. She took my pen to write about her desire to marry, have kids, and be a teacher.

She moved my face close to her cheek so she could feel every word as I read each declaration—feel it the way she had learned to feel the music of the bamboo trees in the prayer garden.

I asked, "Do you want boys or girls?"

She giggled and spoke again. "Two girls. Boys—hard."

Then she wrote on the paper again. "I want to have a big car and house." This time there were no giggles. She closed her eyes to concentrate as she spoke. "I graduate. June."

And in that moment, her dreams and her reality collided. She looked at me with eyes that begged for an answer to the silent question, "And then what?"

Miss Mary cupped my face in her hand, bringing me back to the steamy porch where we were sitting. "It's on you to share our story. It's on you to tell people what you've learned."

She turned to Courtney. "Don't let anything keep her from sharing the story. And if she can't tell it, you need to do it." Courtney looked at me, tears welling. Miss Mary whispered, "The women who read the book—they will learn what happens when we learn to speak."

The students stood proudly as Miss Mary signed, "Are you ready?"

"Happy birthday to you!" filled the room in every language they knew. Hands waved, voices raised, hips moved, feet stomped. Laughter followed—the same big, bold, raucous laughter that first welcomed me to the school years before. Miss Mary had learned the power of the language of love. And she wanted the world to know its power too.

Not long ago, I thought about the kinship that Lisa shares with Miss Mary and Bianca as Lisa and I traveled to Guatemala with a mission team from Orphan Outreach and stood in a government-run home filled with teen moms who had been rescued from sexual exploitation. Spanish was the most common language in the room, though not everyone spoke it. Mayan dialects were there too. Some knew how to read and write, but others had never been given the privilege of education.

Love was the lesson, specifically Romans 8:39: "No power in the sky above or in the earth below—indeed, nothing in all creation will ever be able to separate us from the love of God that is revealed in Christ Jesus our Lord" (NLT).

Members of our mission team held hands with the young women as we stood in straight lines in the center of the cinderblock room. "We're going to share some love. Squeeze the hand of the person to your right," Lisa instructed. The murmur of curious voices rose as, one by one, each person looked at the person to her right and gently squeezed—until there were no hands left. The girls at the end of the lines were crestfallen.

Lisa then moved everyone into a circle. "Let's do this again," she said as she clasped the hands of the girls to her left and right and motioned for the squeezing to begin. "Keep squeezing until you get to the end of the line."

It took only a minute or two before the cautious silence was replaced with giggles. There were no longer empty hands. There was no longer an end. And there was no need for a perfect phrase to explain it. The language of touch had done its work. It was a language Lisa knew well. She spoke it every week to her young moms back home.

The words of the teacher on that muggy morning were the same words I had believed for years. Language was linear, a cause-and-effect formula that relied on voices trained to share well-crafted responses wrapped in eloquence and persuasion. But the Jamaican woman with the big hugs, the Michigan woman unashamed to weep, and the Romanian woman unafraid to let her dialect tell her story had taught me that our God-designed voices are far more like the circle in that Guatemalan government home. They need no perfect pitch, and they have the power to be heard regardless of their volume. They are every accent and every culture and every gentle touch. Miss Mary taught me that love is all the languages, Bianca taught me that heritage is found in our voices, and Lisa taught me that love speaks clearly even when no words are used.

God delights in every nuance of your voice, and your language does its good work when it is the language of those who need to hear.

PART 7

RECLAIMING YOUR COURAGE

I had never ever thought I would be in this place, and it came suddenly. I felt the responsibility was too great—that I couldn't do it. God spoke to me through Scripture—David and Goliath—to trust in Him and not in myself. I received such encouragement. I used to think, *I am doing something for God*. But He told me it is His grace that we are in this ministry, that we are in His kingdom. So there is nothing I can do for God. I simply serve.

from an interview with Joy, director, Dar-Ul-Fazl

> She is strong and graceful,
> as well as cheerful
> about the future.
> Proverbs 31:25 CEV

24

Through the Fire

Each time I travel to La Paz, Honduras, I ask if we can stop by a foundry where aluminum pots are made. We first visited one several years ago, when a local friend asked if we'd like to see a small miracle in the making. Our van wound through narrow streets for a bit, and then we parked next to a rusty corrugated-metal wall. The smell of petroleum and earth was thick in the air, and waves of heat flushed our faces as we entered the yard. On the other side of the wall, men were working—all in tattered clothes and flip-flops. A fire blazing in one corner of the yard transformed recycled metal into brilliant red liquid, and under a thatched roof that offered a bit of shade, the molten metal was poured through small holes in handcrafted molds. Bowls, plates, and large cooking pots were being made that day.

The red-hot aluminum reaches a thousand degrees before it's poured. The laborers' feet and hands are marked with scars—something they say is a harsh reminder of the road marked with purpose.

That first foundry in the community was started by a man who learned the art of casting pots from his grandfather. While there are factories in other parts of the world that make the same types of things, he wanted to retain the heritage and dignity of the craft.

So he set up shop in a struggling neighborhood and made jobs available to men who desperately needed a way to earn a living.

Each item produced means a bit of money in empty pockets, and even more money can be made if the men are willing to travel to the markets. It's difficult work, but the sense of pride in craftsmanship is evident in everyone's faces. The work of their hands feeds their families and pays for electricity and helps start new businesses so more people can work.

There is a rhythm in the well-honed labor of those who cast aluminum, as they shovel dirt into the wooden frames, pack it with their feet, trim away the excess dirt with knives, and carefully examine their work.

Over and over, the process continues.

Shovel, pack, trim, examine.

Two frames are carefully packed, and then the bowl or plate or pot is added and tapped into place with hammers, then even more carefully removed to reveal the shape to come. There is no vocational center or university to teach the laborers; no, everything they have learned has come from the courageous classroom of experience with fire and earth. Scorched earth.

You see, before it can transform the molten metal, the dirt used by the foundry laborers has to undergo its own transformation. It has to go through fire. Only then can it create the pots and pans that will be used to fill bellies and spark life.

The workers walk to a nearby dry riverbed and collect soil. They sift it to remove rocks and debris and then set it ablaze. The fire changes the chemical composition of the soil, making it stronger, more resilient, and more malleable. Only then can it hold its shape and cradle its creation.

The fire gives the soil greater purpose. It gives the soil life. And the soil then gives life to pots that will give life to families that will give life to a community.

I'm amazed by the courage of the men who work in flip-flops to shape the soil and then pour molten metal into its form.

I've shared the story of scorched earth and pots with people who are keen on leadership principles in a culture that thrives on minimizing hardship and maximizing productivity. Most look at me and shake their heads. "Thank God we're past all that. There are far more efficient and less dangerous ways to do things" is the usual response.

I used to nod my head in agreement. But after spending time with the men in the aluminum foundry and the women in this book, I think there's something to be said for the courage to walk through fire rather than walk around it.

Courage taken becomes courage given.

You've met many fire walkers so far. Risk runs deep in the veins of the women who are changing the world in such rich and thoughtful ways. But there are a few more women I want you to meet—women who live and breathe courage in ways I'm just now learning to truly embrace.

25

Elizabeth and Aunty

Her Words Were Her Pledge

There's a first day to every journey. Elizabeth and I shared the same first day. We arrived to the sound of singing—it's always the women singing in Mechimeru, a remote Kenyan village that's closer to Uganda than it is to Kenya's own capital of Nairobi. I remembered Susie's face most that morning, her smile and the way she welcomed us all as she sang, "You are a beautiful flower" in Kiswahili. I arrived by a van that carefully maneuvered the deep, rain-carved ruts of orange clay roads that rarely felt the weight of anything more than bare feet or motorcycles (called *boda-bodas*). Elizabeth followed not too far behind, her business suit and heels seeming quite out of place on the back of the boda-boda.

I was there, at the Madeleine School, to care for a team of doctors and veterinarians and filmmakers. She was there to care for the children. We were both so unsure of our roles. She was the first social worker ever in the village—the first professional to offer counseling and care to students and their families. Orphan Outreach, the ministry in the United States, had seen change in other countries, and so they knew change could come to Kenya too. Elizabeth had seen that change before in the village of Busia, when as a school counselor she had helped children grow strong and bold in setting both goals and boundaries. It was her dream to bring that same program to Bungoma County.

And so on that first day for both of us, we walked the sugarcane fields to visit families and see what change might come. One of the first homes we visited was Susie's. She was still smiling as she invited us into the hut with a single window and a threshold that flooded each time the rains came. A single mom battling AIDS, her greatest love was her two children. They huddled together at night to stay warm against the damp ground, chickens clucking quietly next to them in a basket turned temporary coop.

We talked that day to Susie, Earles the widower, and two grand-mothers who were left to care for little ones after their own children had died of AIDS. I asked about education and child sponsorship and if there were any dreams at all hidden away in homes that had little more than a sleeping mat and an open fire to prepare what little food might be available. And Elizabeth listened carefully to the responses before introducing herself with a simple, "I am Elizabeth, the only wife of one husband. And I am here to care for you now at Madeleine School."

Her words were her pledge.

Working in Mechimeru wasn't the only first for Elizabeth. It was also the first time in the history of her marriage that she and her husband lived in the same village. "In Kenya, you must go where there are jobs. So for fourteen years, we have not had the privilege of being in the same village. There was a season we weren't even in the same country. Now we are together. And we are glad."

Elizabeth's first day has become a reminder to me never to be afraid to say yes to the first days, the new steps, the uncharted territory, the unpaved path.

I said my farewell to Kenya, and she set about getting to know every child at Madeleine School. And she never stopped walking in those sugarcane fields to visit the families. It's in the homes that she's able to speak candidly about what she's seen and heard from the children. "In our school, we deal with those children who have lost one or both parents, and those who are in very vulnerable groups because of poverty and abuse. Most of them are traumatized; some are confused. They need to be loved, they need the love of a parent, they need a lot of encouragement to put the pieces together again."

The next time I saw Elizabeth she was smiling. Gone were the heels that didn't travel well in sugarcane fields, and the calendar on her desk was filled with the names of students and families who were attending therapy sessions. "Do you remember what a great plan I had when I arrived, Madame?" She laughed. She calls me Madame—a gesture of the highest respect. The children may call me Aunty or Tia or Ron, and the men call me Sister, but Elizabeth calls me Madame.

She had a great plan, with curriculum and activities that would help children learn to prepare for the future and care for themselves. But those plans were replaced by the reality of living in a community where teaching the most fundamental of life skills is lifesaving to a child. Elizabeth began teaching self-awareness, about being bold without changing who God made them to be. She and the students talked about preventing bullying and abuse, about puberty and the changes taking place in their bodies, about healthy relationships. She learned all there was to know about Kenyan law, and she added it to her lessons.

"We talk about the difference between defilement and rape. No, there is really no difference other than age," she said. "But the children must know what to do in case of any danger, in case of any abuse. They must know how to protect themselves, how to always walk in groups, how to always watch out for each other. They must know how predators think and what predators do. They are taught to tell caregivers and social workers about any harm that has come to them, even the threat of defilement. And I teach them to scream. At any sense of danger, I teach them to scream loudly—and not to stop until they can tell the authorities. No one has the rights to their bodies."

There are no phones in the homes to call 911. Electricity is a luxury. Screaming sounds the alarm and alerts others.

Elizabeth knows that teaching the children does not go unseen by the adults. She's received praise from many parents, but the threats have been present too. Elizabeth doesn't let them deter her. In fact, if anything, the opposition has made her stronger.

Just like the fire in the foundry.

Something True and Real

A few thousand miles to the east you'll find Aunty. She has walked through more fire than anyone I've met in my life. Her story could honestly be the screenplay for an epic suspense thriller, and the things I could write about her life would take up chapters instead of pages. So if you'll offer a little extra grace, I'm going to share only pieces of her journey so that I can focus more on what she's taught me about being courageous in the face of seemingly insurmountable odds.

She wasn't always called Aunty. Her grandfather named her Romawii, which means "beautiful treasure" in her native language of Mizo. Her grandfather was one of the first Christians in her homeland, and he delighted in traveling to villages to share the love of Jesus. Aunty says God blessed him for his work by giving the family one of the first homes with a real tin roof. It was her grandfather's faith that inspired Aunty to leave all that was familiar to find her heart's passion. That passion led her to children—the children who would call her Aunty, a term of the fondest affection and trust.

"In my life, I have to believe that I am doing what God has called me to do. I don't have a lot to be proud about—education or wealth. But God has always been with me and given me favor."

Aunty is a reserved, gracious woman in her seventies who cares far more about the fine details and comfort of others than she does about herself. I first fell in love with her while watching her worship with her children as the sun rose over the foothills of the Himalayas.

I walked into her living room, tucked away near the entrance to Dar-Ul-Fazl ("House of Grace"), and found afternoon light shining through lace curtains, a stack of Bibles on a side table, and a fragrance reminiscent of attics filled with treasures. She motioned for me to sit. "You might be very tired—you traveled yesterday whole day. Are you get good night's rest? Sit anywhere you like." I sat down in the chair closest to the front door, and she frowned. She motioned again—this time for me to come closer, to a sofa near her so we could hear each other over the laughter of the children outside, a consistent soundtrack to the day. "I love the sound of their laughter and singing," she said in broken English. "My heart is filled of joy."

Because of her family's Christian heritage, Aunty was well acquainted with the fire of faith. But she wasn't expecting the fires of persecution to burn so strongly.

In her early thirties, she traveled more than one thousand miles by herself from the state of Mizoram in India to the former state of Jammu and Kashmir to share the gospel. The first few years were quiet, then she and her team were attacked by a Muslim sect that was hostile to the gospel. "We would often be beaten up, our books were burnt, and our bicycles smashed and damaged." Aunty and her friends began praying about how best to serve the community and live out their love of Christ without hostility, and she felt called by God to open a home for children under the age of six. She wanted to provide sanctuary and a little hope.

As we sat together, she paused for a moment and then looked at me intently. "I never worry for my future. God is with me all the time. When He asked me to start the home, we had no money and no support. But we had Him."

House of Grace was founded in 1982 in Srinagar, Kashmir. At first, villagers were afraid of the home, saying they would rather have children starve to death than risk being ostracized by their community for living with Christians.

"We began to pray fervently that the Lord would give us children. One afternoon as we were still praying, there was a knock on the door. I opened the door softly since the others were still praying. A man was there; he told me he had heard about our home and wondered if we had space to take in children from his hometown in Ladakh." Three days later, Aunty and her staff traveled to Ladakh to meet the children. "When we arrived, there were lots of children and their parents waiting for us. The parents told us, 'Madamji, please hurry and take our children. We need to get to work or else we will not have money to buy food for even today.' We had not enough room for all the children, so we said we would take those who were youngest first." Even then, Aunty had no way of transporting the children back to House of Grace. So she prayed again that God would provide. There was another knock at the door. The next day Aunty and eighteen children traveled in a donated tourist bus to their new home.

The children's home quickly grew as word got out about the quality of care provided for the children. But not everyone was happy about a Christian children's home in a Buddhist state. In 1988, members of the Buddhist Leaders Association demanded the home be closed and the fifty-four Ladakhi children be returned to their hometown. "We traveled with the children back to Leh, Ladakh, and sat in the center of the town as the claims against us were read. The Buddhist Leaders Association secretary said that the children in the home preferred the gospel to the teachings of the Dalai Lama, which could destroy Buddhism in their village. It was decided that the children had to be removed from the home to protect Ladakh from Christianity."

Aunty and her staff returned to an empty House of Grace. Beds were untouched, food was in the pantry, and she wept for her children. As she prayed, she recalled Isaiah 49:20: "You will again hear the children who were born bereaved say, 'The place is too crowded for me; make room for me to settle'" (CEB). And slowly, House of Grace became home for other orphaned and vulnerable children from different states.

In 1990, border terrorism escalated, and the safety of the children became an issue, so House of Grace moved four hundred miles to the south, to the Manali area in the state of Himachal Pradesh. Aunty opened Rainbow School, a place to educate not only the children in her home but those in the village as well. Both Hindus and Christians welcomed the children and their caregivers, and even the president of India met with Aunty and the children and gave his blessing on the good work being done. The acceptance was fresh breath to Aunty, but she still grieved the loss of her Ladakhi children.

What she didn't know was that a small group of those children had learned from her courage, and they were on their way to find her. Joy, one of the original House of Grace children who now serves as director for the home, knew she had to return. "My friend and I talked often about how we wanted to return to Aunty. She had shown us love and care, and there was something about it that was true and real. We had to do our morning prayers, so we would bow down before Buddha and pray to Jesus. Those prayers gave us bravery, and we decided to plan our escape." Six children found their way back to Aunty, many with parents who risked their own lives for the sake of their children.

26

Take Courage

Aunty has been unafraid to walk through fire. Elizabeth is much like her. Both women have moxie, but neither is fearless. Their lives and their leadership are powerful reminders that true courage doesn't rise in the absence of fear but rather in the midst of it. I can't help but think of a woman who Catholics have named Veronica. She is unnamed in Scripture, but you might know her as the bleeding woman.

> Just then a woman who had hemorrhaged for twelve years slipped in from behind and lightly touched his robe. She was thinking to herself, "If I can just put a finger on his robe, I'll get well." Jesus turned—caught her at it. Then he reassured her: "Courage, daughter. You took a risk of faith, and now you're well." The woman was well from then on. (Matt. 9:20–22)

There it is. Courage.

Jesus turned, looked the woman in the eye, and said, "Courage, daughter." He didn't say, "Hey, girl, slap that fear in the face and get your act together or you can forget about getting anything from Me." No, He saw her there, trembling and yet taking the next step. He smiled and looked her in the eye as if she were the only one on the road. And He told her to take courage.

I wonder how many doctors examined the woman with the bleeding and tried to figure out what was wrong. How many prescriptions was she given to make things better, how many conflicting diagnoses did she hear, how many times did she hear the whispers of "crazy" or "bringing this on herself" or "all in her head"?

She must have felt every emotion over the twelve years. She must have blamed everything and everyone—including God and herself—at least once when things didn't get better. Chances are things *did* get better for short seasons, and her hope grew—only to be dashed when the blood started flowing again. She must have felt so much shame, must have felt so alone, wondering, *Is there anyone at all like me?* I bet at some point she wished she would simply disappear—because being treated like you're invisible is such a painful way to live.

I wish we knew what happened to the woman after she took courage and felt life rise within her, what happened after the bleeding stopped and shame was destroyed. I wonder how many people doubted her story, how many doctors tried to take credit for something only Love could do, how often the "crazy" or "bringing this on herself" or "all in her head" thoughts came back, trying to steal the truth. I wonder how many times she took fresh courage and how many times her courage was used to shape the lives of others.

Yes, Catholics gave the woman a name.[1] They call her Veronica. It means "true image." It also means "she who brings victory." I know the meanings because it's my given name. I think about those meanings often and pray my life will one day reflect them fully. Those meanings most certainly describe Elizabeth and Aunty—and the other women who believe restoration is a reality in their communities and their countries.

Maybe we're all like Veronica in a way—all carrying questions and pain, scars and stains and shame, and all invited to take courage from the Savior and Lord who knows both our frailty and our fortitude, who knows the impact our lives will have when we take Him at His word.

Scripture says that power left Jesus's body when He healed the woman who had been bleeding for years. In my mind, I picture her literally receiving courage from Jesus in that power. I believe the same for Elizabeth and Aunty. They have, time and time again, taken courage from Jesus. And the courage they have received gives courage to those around them.

The courage Elizabeth has received in the village filled with questions, scars, and pain has emboldened her. "What keeps me going is that I really love these children, and I will do anything at any moment to make sure they are well settled and safe and healthy. The moment I see them in a not-good situation, I can't rest until I can help. As a mother, sometimes it makes me feel bad, because I choose to put on those shoes and take on the children at the school as my own children, so whatever abuses are happening to those children feel like they're happening to my family. I feel like I should go after anything to see that the abuse ends."

What Aunty has learned about the purpose of fire and about the power of courage she passes on to the eighty children who call House of Grace their true home these days. There is no such thing as "aging out" in Aunty's eyes, and there's rarely a day when college students or young professionals aren't visiting the home. Her philosophy of care for the children at House of Grace and for the students at Rainbow School is steeped in grace and love, and she is revered by every staff member and child.

Her advice for raising children is summed up in three words: fear the Lord. "The fear of the Lord is the beginning of wisdom," she shared with a smile. "Those who fear the Lord will flee from sin. Whatever we can do, we do. We share grace and love. We adopt the children in our hearts. We cannot force anything, and so we pray. I want my children not to be nominal Christians. My hope is that they'll all be strong. I know that may not be a reality, but it is my hope. I pray they remember all they've learned. I pray they'll see they can't find the true God in Hinduism, or Buddhism, or Islam. They will one day return to their villages and face all sorts of things. We want them to remain faithful. It makes me happy when I am told, 'We face big problems, but we have decided to face our problems with God and prayer. We choose Christ.'"

27

Courage Taken Becomes Courage Given

In Busia, Elizabeth had a job. At the Madeleine School, it's become her calling. Courage has done that. She is not the same Elizabeth who arrived by boda-boda that September day in 2014. She has been refined by fire, and its glow surrounds her.

We sat under the shelter of a tin roof as the children outside squealed their delight at a sudden downpour. She closed her eyes and took in the sounds and the fragrance of African farmland kissed by the sky. Then she looked at me, her eyes glistening.

"When I was in Busia, it was so hard. But this, this is different."

And then she laughed.

"I'm sure if you look at me, you see that I'm not the same now. I mean, I am the same woman, but I'm not the same. I feel settled. And settling is not just a house and a given point in time. No, settling is all around. God has kept me in His care and helped me find my place, and He's helped me when I struggle with how to balance work and family and counseling and time. It's not my own making—it's God's grace. I have truly found the depths of God's grace now.

"And Orphan Outreach has helped settle me. I have been given a home in an organization. I think about before—I was in pieces.

I was unsettled; I felt so alone in my efforts to help others, and I felt overwhelmed with the problems all around me. But I have a team now. A team. And that has helped me so much."

She laughed again.

"I am happy. And that has even improved my health as well. And it's been a great help to my family and children. My family can have both parents together—father and mother together settled in one place. And my time here at the school with the children is helping me be a better mother in my own home. There are times you'll walk in my home and there are so many children from the neighborhood, and you'll think, *Oh my gosh, are these all her children?* But somehow all the neighborhood children really find solace at our home. So I think perhaps I've become a better mother to my own children, and I've become now the mother of our community.

"The time I spend with my family and my children helps me to better think of ways we can improve our services here at the school and in this community. I think about how we can better care for children from conception forward. We can't merely look at what we are doing on the outside of a child. We must look at how we are treating a child from the womb and throughout their life."

There in the rain-washed green and clay of Kenya, Elizabeth has a new dream. But this dream isn't a program or an activity. The fire has sparked a way of life for the place she calls home.

"I used to have a dream of educating the children—that education would help change lives. But now I see that it's more than education. It's lifestyle. And when I talk about lifestyle, it won't take a day, but it will come. I feel that in the future, God willing—because everything is out of God's making—I want to see the lifestyle of these children change, physically and socially and spiritually and emotionally. We've already boarded this train—it's going—and so it will happen. I see a place flying high above the standard here, a place where children are proud and lives are changed and our community is changed because of it. Oh, and in my dream, these children learn and grow and then come back to be a great help to their own parents. They become business leaders, and they become teachers. They uplift the lifestyle of their families, making homes safer and improving the environment and ensuring safety."

As her words tumbled out, the sun broke through the storm clouds. In Kiswahili, there is a word for that moment. *Kianga.* Elizabeth's heart for the students and their families is kianga—the first sunlight breaking through the darkness.

The children ran to the field to play football in the damp grass, and Elizabeth waved her approval. "Even if I get so tired, so worn-out, so burned-out, despite all the happenings, I've made a change in the kids' lives, and that makes me feel more alive each day and every moment."

Aunty's now retired from House of Grace, but she remains a very strong presence at both the home and the school. She has seen so many dreams fulfilled over the years that she struggles to create a new list of wishes. There's the hope that Rainbow School will expand to twelfth grade so more children may be served and, in turn, grow up learning to serve the poor and vulnerable. She would love to see her House of Grace kids return to their villages and open schools and children's homes. And she thinks it would be nice to have a reunion for all those who have left the home to pursue careers, ministry, and family.

But she believes in dreaming big—and the woman in her seventies has no intention of quitting. Her ministry efforts have expanded beyond the walls of House of Grace to Manali and neighboring villages. "We are working to see how we might look after poor families, those who cannot go to college. We asked ourselves how we might develop a training center, with computers, so we can teach life skills and basic labor training to make them less vulnerable. In India, trafficking is strong. Children are purchased, and the traffickers deceive the parents by telling them that they will take the children to a good school. The children are then sold into slavery—primarily sexual slavery. We must give women strength."

I looked at the demure woman on the sofa next to me and, for a moment, I imagined the sweet scent of smoke perfuming her. "I have times I am sad or afraid, but then I see what God is doing. And now I am helping women to understand their rights. And that gives me hope. I am not an expert, but God is with me. The children feel I am their mother, and the women are feeling that too. And that's why so many women come to learn. They want help. They want someone who will fight for them. We are learning and we are doing. We have to walk for this kind of thing—we have to step and step again in our faith. Some people don't want to hear that because they just want things. But we have learned that we have to live our faith. We raise our faith by learning and by doing."

Aunty stopped and looked at her left hand, remembering a question I had asked long before we talked about raising children or protecting women. "You asked me about my singleness. I want to make sure I respond to you because it is important that women know it is not a bad thing to be single."

Aunty will tell you that marriage is an expectation in her country. While laws protecting women's rights are becoming more prevalent, regard for women in leadership is still limited. Aunty's father was worried about her. Her mother prayed. But Aunty knew her life would be different than her culture demanded; there would be no husband who would join her in ministry. "My uncle was much like my father," she said. "He would tell me, 'If you are not married, who will look after you? You'll be an old woman all alone. You will suffer.' My father said, 'Go and do ministry—you can still get married after you get old.' But he then said that whatever I said God had told me to do, I had to do.

"I told my family, 'I have assurance of salvation in Christ, and I am sure of my calling. Until I drop to the ground dead, God will be with me and He will not make me ashamed. He will never lose me.' I thought there might be some regret after time, but God chose me to choose Him. And I've never regretted. I am happy to be single, and God has given me a lot of children. I don't hesitate to say my husband is Jesus Christ. In all my lifetime, I am sure God wants me and He has called me.

"Be sure that He will never leave you and that He will provide whatever you need. Look around me. I have all this family. Our family is who God has said. There is no reason to be afraid. We have no need to fear. Let's take courage in our God."

To encourage means to stand by someone, to help them take the next step. When Jesus told the woman to take courage, He didn't then turn and walk away. He demonstrated courage by encouraging, by giving courage. Even when His own life became the one filled with questions, accusations, scars, and pain. Even when He felt the flames of persecution, oppression, and fear. Even when He became the one whose blood poured out to redeem the world.

Yes, courage taken becomes courage given. Aunty and Elizabeth don't have to be fearless. They are fire walkers. And they have taught me to be unafraid of the fire, for it's there that new purpose and new power are found.

Embrace that God-breathed, Christ-offered, Spirit-infused courage, and let it strengthen backs, strengthen legs, strengthen hands and hearts—yours and those of the people who are changed because of the courage you then give.

Take courage, fire walker.

PART 8

RECLAIMING YOUR IDENTITY

You have a unique voice in all the world, a singular calling, a distinct destiny. God created you for it, and it really doesn't matter how you compare with someone else. Just like Jesus told Peter after the resurrection, when he was all worked up about what Jesus was calling John to do. With an uncompromising answer, Jesus gently put Peter firmly in his place with these words: "If I will that he remain until I come, what is that to you? You follow Me" (John 21:22).

from *The God Dare* by Kate Battistelli

She looks over a field and buys it,
then, with money she's put aside, plants a garden.

Proverbs 31:16–17

28

Our Own Worst Enemy

"I pray that no one ever looks at my life and says, 'That girl—
you know, she always played it safe.'" I wrote those words after
returning from a season of travel in which I spent time with yet
more women who turned my faith even further on its head with
their boldly quiet and bravely effectual love for Jesus. I don't want
to be a safe girl.

I have a feeling you're like me in that way. You want to be unafraid to be you too. I want you to be you. That's what every word,
every story, every page of this book is about. It's about you reclaiming all of God's beautifully crafted physical, emotional, intellec-
tual, and spiritual DNA. It's about you looking in the mirror and
saying with quiet confidence, "I am a woman, and all that I am is
wonderful."

But chances are there have been moments when you've read one
of the stories and thought, *Well, if I lived in a foreign land, I'd
be able to make a difference too.* Or *If I was younger (or older),
married (or single), funnier or smarter or wealthier, more creative,
less encumbered, more like them and less like me . . .*

Every one of the women in this book has battled the same thing.
In the first chapter, I said that the real enemy of us is *us*. It's the
way we view ourselves in light of the way we view others. It's the

way we rank ideals of beauty, talent, giftedness, purpose—and always place ourselves slightly lower than others. If we are our worst enemy, then I believe comparison is our most destructive weapon. Comparison rarely moves us to contentment. Rather, it pushes us toward competition or condemnation—or a fierce ping-pong match of both.

I've only traveled to St. Petersburg, Russia, in the winter, when the skies struggle to wake up before ten and are already darkening by early afternoon. Canal ways fill with ice floes, and radiators in even the nicest hotels war with the damp cold outside. The city streets wind and connect like rivers, with every major thoroughfare leading back to statues of Peter the Great.

Peter was hungry to make his namesake city famous. He traveled throughout Europe in the late 1600s, taking note of style and nuance. He wanted his city to be known as the window to Europe, the Venice of the north. He was so entranced with the idea of creating something more magnificent than all the magnificent somethings in other countries that he forgot to focus on the unique qualities of his own homeland.

St. Petersburg was built on thirty-two islands. More than three hundred bridges connect pieces of the city. Originally, Peter had visions of using all that water to mimic the canals of his Italian neighbor. *His* watery paradise would be bigger and better.

And so it was. Until winter came. In a city that's as far north as Alaska, streets made of water don't fare well in the bitter cold. Prior to that first winter, watery canals they were. But those canals froze. When spring came, waterways were filled with cobblestone and concrete. Peter's dream became a symbol of what happens when we forget the beauty of our own identities.

Peter allowed comparison to fuel fierce competition and reckless risk. I, on the other hand, have at times abandoned risk by allowing comparison to feed my own condemnation. But risk that celebrates our unique identities is powerful and life changing. Culture may find its joy in capturing our attention with comparison and fueling competition and condemnation in the process. Our childhood dreams may be seen as foolish, our present-day circumstances may not be ideal, but our lives are purposeful. And the most important thing we can embrace about our God-designed influence and impact is our God-created identities.

29

Elena

Everything Happens for a Reason

As a little girl with thick glasses and a lisp from sucking my finger until I was nine, I longed to be an archaeologist and a mom to orphans because "kids need love too." Adults at the time smiled, rolled their eyes, and said, "How cute." No one in my family cared much about digging up old stories, and no one was involved in orphan care ministry. Besides reading *Little Orphan Annie* and *Charlotte's Web*, I knew nothing about living with a family that wasn't yours by birth. But I did understand what it felt like to be abused and rejected. And I didn't think it was right for that to happen to anyone.

Elena had a childhood dream too. In fact, she had many of them. When I first met her, she had just celebrated her sixteenth birthday, and our conversation was a patchwork quilt of basketball games and school and wishing she was twelve again because "you don't have to worry about anything when you're twelve."

Sixteen for Elena meant maneuvering a car through the cramped, winding streets of Sololá, her hometown that is tucked away in the volcanic hills that surround Lake Atitlan in Guatemala. In many ways, she was like any other teenager. When a group of young women from the United States pitied her because she didn't have the luxury of good shopping and a movie theater, she shook her head and laughed. "Seriously? I have a great life. I do what teenagers do. I read, I hang out with my friends, I spend too much time on social media. I do stuff with my family. Do you do stuff with your family?" Pizza and French fries were her favorite foods back then, and she couldn't stop giggling when boys became part of the conversation. She loved good music and studying English, but not math, and she thought it might be fun to be a singer-songwriter when she grew up.

So what did a sixteen-year-old worry about, anyway? She smiled when I asked. "School and stuff. I hate the fact that I'm going to finish school, because I love school. The best days were when I was little and I wanted to be on the big kids' side of things. And now I'm here. It feels heavy and serious. But it's cool."

I remember wanting to be on the big kids' side of things too. And I agree with Elena. It does often feel heavy and serious on this side. But each decade brings fresh grace and many lovely lessons with it. Yes, it's pretty cool.

Elena was born in Guatemala. The only house she knows is the one owned by the generations before her, and she's never experienced life without her grandparents. "I was with my great-grandmother when she died. She lived with us until her very last day on this earth. We didn't send her away or put her in a home. We were all there, holding her hand and praying for her when she took her last breath. That's what we do. We're *family*. That's why I know my grandmother worries about what happens when I go out on my own. I'm the first grandchild and the only granddaughter.

"It really hit me just how different my life is from other kids' lives when my grandmother in Canada—my mom's mom—got sick, and we had to move her to an old folks' house. I wasn't used to people kicking their family into other places. It was then I realized just how different the cultures are that I live in. Oh my gosh, I *am* different from the other kids. I get to have one foot in each culture."

Elena was young, but she had already witnessed the continued struggle with prejudice in the world around her. She believed embracing heritage rather than fighting it might provide hope. Her own family tree has branches that have been splintered by bloody history.

"My great-great-great-grandparents were Spaniards—the ones who came to Guatemala to war with the indigenous Mayans and claim the country as their own. Their child was called a *criollo*, a Guatemalan child of parents from another country. If that child married an indigenous Guatemalan and had a child, that child was called a *mestizo*, a mix of Spaniard and indigenous. That was my great-grandmother, Marta. She married an indigenous Guatemalan and had my grandmother, Sylvia. I am proud to claim both mestizo and criollo as my heritage.

"I know everything happens for a reason—even bad things—and if the Spaniards hadn't come here, we wouldn't be here. Some people are ashamed because of the damage the Spaniards inflicted. People who don't see the past as the past think it's embarrassing to include that past in your heritage. Some are embarrassed to say they're Mayan because they believe it means they are primitive and incapable of learning. That is such a lie. I am Spaniard, and I am Mayan. My past is part of who I am, but my past doesn't have to define my present or my future."

Rich in What Counts

During high school Elena and her friends were passionate about cultural diversity and caring for those who struggle to survive. Her normally bright face grew dim as she recounted the stories of Guatemalans risking their lives to travel northward to a place they'd been told offered opportunity and freedom.

"When I go to Canada or the US with my family and I meet an immigrant, it's so amazing, because it's like, 'You're my people!'

I get so frustrated with those who speak badly about immigrants. Oh my gosh, they're just trying to make a life for their families. The United States invites people to dream dreams and live life. And people believe that. And then they are told they're not welcome. And that's horrible. Who does that?

"And then the United States sends people to our country and says we are poor and we need help—we need Jesus. We are pitied, and we are told we need to be like them. Here's the thing—we are the rich ones. We are rich in what counts."

I asked her if she remembered the night we drove in the back of a pickup truck to her home—the night she was asked so many questions by so many people about what it was like to live in a hard place without great luxuries like movie theaters and easy access to the best shopping. Her brow furrowed. "I do remember one thing I said. That I don't believe money defines riches and not having it defines poverty. You know, sometimes I believe the US may be the poorest nation. I think they may need Jesus most of all."

What has always counted to Elena is her faith and family. She was one of only a handful of Christians who attended her high school. "People assume that because we're a religious country there would be many kids eager to serve Christ. But that's not reality. It gets lonely sometimes, and I'm thankful for the friends I do have. But my purpose isn't to hang out with Christians. It's to be an example to those who aren't. Some have been raised in Christian homes but don't want to embrace it. Some have parents who have been hurt by Christians from our country or other countries. Some have parents who have recently changed their lives, but their past continues to haunt the children.

"Even teachers don't want to talk about religion. But it's still a big topic. And so I'll speak out. I believe they'll see the reality of Jesus when I live out my faith in front of them."

And it's that faith that had Elena thinking about the future in the midst of basketball and Instagram and boys. "I want to travel everywhere, but I want to set my home where people speak

Spanish. I want my family to be here. Because there's a connection in Latin America. And it's here I want to create a place for old people to live out their days well."

As a teen, Elena already had a dream of creating a space for the elderly—not a nursing home like her grandmother's in Canada—because "families need to care for families." Her space would be for those who have no one, for those who have been abandoned, for those who have no family. She once told me, "I want a place where they will be loved and cared for, where they'll be able to laugh and enjoy life and teach others."

Her eyes glistened, and I saw a distant dream come to life in her eyes. "Old people have wisdom. They have stories. They are the history we read about. We chase to care for babies, and we think kids are cool, but we walk away when people grow old. And they still have life to share. Oh my gosh, I know there are people who have been through wars and have survived. I know they're here for us, and they have insight on so much. They can help our future."

Even as a teen, Elena's life was different from the lives of most of her friends. There were options. Her father was Guatemalan, and her mother was Canadian, so Elena had dual citizenship. She was fluent in English and Spanish, and she understood the colloquial nuances of the Mayan culture deeply infused in the people who tend to the land and shop at the open-air market and care for their families in homes often lacking electricity or running water.

When we first met, she helped translate for me at a children's home and school a few miles away from her home. Though the singer-songwriter idea was a fun one, something happened to Elena the first time she was asked to help bridge languages and cultures. She found a voice that went deeper than translating words. She discovered a passion in translating hope.

At sixteen, she wasn't sure exactly where that passion would take her, but she couldn't shake it. She knew there was a place for her different life. And she wanted her different life to make life different for others.

30

The Truth about Comparison

In Genesis 1, God made it all. He spoke sunlight and shade and stars and sea into their places. A most amazing Creator used His imagination, crafted His creation, and gave it life. It flew, ran, scampered. Everything reflected His glory—every color, every sound, every texture. He looked at all He had done and declared it good.

And then I picture Him taking another look and saying, "And yet there's something missing."

That something would be love wrapped in flesh and bone. While God spoke other pieces of His creation into being, He carefully and tenderly handcrafted man and woman. He infused His own character into each of them, animated them with His own breath in their lungs, and placed them in an environment where they could thrive. "Now, this—*this* is very good!" He proclaimed.

Much is said about sin being born in a bite of fruit. But I think it really crawled its way into the life of Adam and Eve with the first hint of comparison. There in a garden where God Himself delighted in long strolls and good conversations about the day, in a world without swimsuit seasons or sickness or sorrow, both

Adam and Eve decided their identities were lacking. The voice of comparison took their contentment and turned it upside down. It dared to claim God's provision was inadequate, His goodness lacking, His gifts withheld.

If you've read Scripture, you know the rest of the story, of God's great fidelity in the midst of our wandering and wondering, of His relentless, restorative love as we question and deny and walk in circles and walk away, of His complete salvation through the life, death, and resurrection of Jesus Christ.

And if you're like me, comparison is always wanting to catch your eye, to shift your attention from an identity designed by God and made complete in Christ to an identity defined by pride, fear, insecurity, or shame. Comparison becomes the sin-filled weapon threatening to kill, steal, and destroy the goodness of our own stories.

Recently, I had to confess to a friend of mine that I was jealous of her life because it made for a better story than mine (in my opinion). No, it wasn't that she lived a more adventurous or glamorous existence. Rather, KJ battles daily with the debilitating effects of an autoimmune disorder. That's right. I was jealous of her *sickness*. Comparison is an insidious beast. Thankfully, she was gracious in her response, confessing her own battles with jealousy. "You know," she said, "sin is anything we do that rejects our lives as the place where God is present, that makes us reject what we've been given and call it 'not good.'"

In Genesis 1, God handcrafted us and called us His prize, the apple of His eye. He created us to be "strong helper standing face-to-face." He looked at us and called us "very good." And He has not changed His mind. Our stories and our identities are divinely inspired.

> For we are the product of His hand, heaven's poetry etched on lives, created in the Anointed, Jesus, to accomplish the good works God arranged long ago. (Eph. 2:10 VOICE)

■ ■ ■ ■

There's nothing I like more than when fragrance permeates the air—like the angel's share in the aging room of the Jack Daniel's whiskey distillery, or the hint of smoke and moss that accompanies a fireplace on a chilly winter's evening, or the scent of warm vanilla and sugar that greets you at the San Martin bakeries in Guatemala. I would have loved to have been with Jesus the night Mary shattered an alabaster bottle and poured expensive perfume on His feet. Scripture says the pleasant fragrance filled the room, and no one could escape it.

Something powerful happens in you and me when we see ourselves as uniquely designed with intention and purpose. I want you to consider what happens when you simply see yourself—*every bit* of your identity—as God-breathed. I think it's a lot like the distillery or the bakery. We become like perfume.

Mother Teresa jotted down some words about sacrifice in a diary as she prepared for her first journey to India as a young woman. She was simply going to serve as an assignment—with no idea that this first trip would ultimately lead to a life in India, or how the work of her hands and heart would inspire millions, or how her nickname would one day be "the little Bride of Christ in the world." Maybe she felt the sacrifice was leaving the creature comforts of home, or walking away from the idea of courtship and marriage because she had chosen to be a nun, or stepping away from something that might have been far more attractive or popular, or perhaps sailing into a great and vulnerable unknown.

She wrote that she chose differently than the cultural norms in her country because she knew there was something about her design that would be compromised otherwise. She wrote about the pain and that she believed it was a sacrifice worth making without even knowing its outcome. And I believe that when young Teresa chose to journey to India because of her love for Christ and her understanding of His love for her, the fragrance filled the room.

That gives me comfort—knowing there will be sacrifices I will make, things I will lay down, choices and decisions that to others might be invisible or insane or inane, and yet the Lord knows and is ever faithful to encourage and to walk the road because He sees the me that was designed specifically to bring honor and glory to Him. Embracing our God-given identities doesn't keep the temptation of comparison away, but it unshackles us from its bondage. He *sees* us—beautiful and unfettered.

31

God-Designed and God-Breathed

A few years ago, I wrote an article to encourage women to be unafraid to try new things no matter the season of their lives. "It's okay to ask, 'Where do I feel truly and fully alive?'" I shared. "Where could I dwell for the longest of times? Where does my heart find its home?" I still have days when comparison rears its head, but I still believe our greatest dreams are in the places that feel like home to us. So I'm taking my own advice. Let's find bravery to embrace our identities and pursue our dreams, even if we're shaking a bit. Sometimes we just need to do something that scares the holy bejeebers out of us.

Now in her twenties, Elena is doing just that. A college student pursuing her business degree, she laughs at the thought of doing something that seems almost disruptive to the life she'd been living. "I mean, what is this? I thought I'd maybe go to seminary or something. A business degree? Me? Math. Whatever."

After graduating high school, while her friends were planning for college and discussing futures that included marriage and families, Elena joined Youth with a Mission. The passion born in her cross-cultural life and the fire to burn through boundaries shined brightly as she traveled abroad to serve refugees. "God was so huge in it all. Every day I would wake up and ask Him to take me to the right people so that I could care for them and pray for them. And every day I would hear Him say, 'Stand here' or 'Go to this certain street,' and I would, and then people would show up and I would talk to them and they would tell me about their brokenness. And we would pray. I saw God heal people. I saw God save people. He isn't stopped by culture. He isn't stopped by country boundaries. He isn't stopped by us."

She then moved to the United States and Canada for a bit, continuing to focus on building cultural bridges while her dream of returning to her homeland grew. The college she attends is in Sololá. She's still bridge building as a translator for Orphan Outreach. There's nothing she loves more than praying for strangers as faith rises and healing comes. And she has not given up on her dream to serve the elderly in Guatemala. The business degree will help her get there.

"I don't have it all figured out already," she said. "I mean, oh man, it's a little scary, right? But God made me this way, and so He knows how I am. I don't want to be anybody else. That's no fun."

Elena has been a great role model when it comes to identity. We don't live in the same neighborhood, and I could honestly be her grandmother (albeit a young one, but still a grandmother), yet she reminds me every time we talk that a woman living in the Texas Hill Country can change the world simply by being herself.

Elena's enthusiasm about seeing her God-designed identity unfold has encouraged me to embrace every piece of my own story.

The little girl with thick glasses and a lisp grew up to be a woman who found success in doing things in which stories could be told but found herself *most* at home in places many folks thought were broken beyond repair. A friend named Amy was the first person to see the longing within me to tell stories of hope and she encouraged me to move from the comfort of the corporate world to the wilds of a nonprofit. The road was rougher than I thought it would be, and there were days I shook and looked back at the trappings of the life I had known, wondering if I had made a huge mistake. But along the way, I met others who saw the childhood dream coming to life in me—a dream no longer considered cute or silly. Instead, it was seen as my unique design.

It's been more than a decade since I took that first step away from telling stories to get people to buy a DVD or tune in to a television show. Archaeology is more about discovering the real story buried under dirt and diesel than it is about brushing the dust from bones, and my God-crafted family has grown huge through child sponsorship and friendship and being an "Aunty."

There's a little army of people on the rough road with me now—folks I've met in countries all over the world and folks I've met drinking a cup of the best chai ever on a Monday afternoon. Don't get me wrong—there are still times I wonder if the stories I'm now telling are making a difference, and there are days when the memories of a time when things were bigger, brighter, and bolder tempt me to compare, compete, and condemn. There are days I shake a bit.

But then I remember that eternity lives in me, in my God-breathed identity.

Elena keeps encouraging me to keep my eyes focused on all that God has created in this body, mind, heart, and soul. As she says, "I don't want to be anybody else. That's no fun."

There is no need to look elsewhere for a unique design. There is no need to compare or compete or condemn. We are God-designed and God-breathed. Eternity lives in us, and that is a most worthy identity to embrace.

Epilogue

It's been a decade since I stood with the clouds at my feet and fell in love with the work of Lourdes and Teresa, the two sisters in Quetzaltenango, Guatemala.

And it's been four years since Miss Mary asked, "What are you waiting for?"

Oh, Miss Mary. The fiery woman whose faith in the unseen taught me how substantive faith really is. It was in her words that I saw *all* the women—those I knew and those I hadn't yet met. It was in her words that I discovered my own longing to become a woman who believes restoration can be a reality on earth as it is in heaven.

Does anyone truly know where a story begins? And does anyone know where—or if—it ever ends?

What I've learned from the women who lead with grace continues to teach me, to change me, to transform my journey. Perhaps that's the way it is with stories. Perhaps that's the way it should be. We learn, we grow, we rise and fall and rise again, and our stories become the catalyst for someone else's story.

A Fighting Kind of Hope

Not long ago, a small team of people from the US joined me to work in Mathare Slum, the second-largest and most impoverished slum in Nairobi that has a population of around 750,000 people. We stepped over ditches filled with raw sewage and held hands as we walked to the homes of students who attend Patmos Junior School. A small bag of groceries seemed such an insignificant gift to give to the mothers and grandmothers who rise before dawn to quilt together scraps of care for their little ones. Poverty is always there, in the slums and the villages no matter the country, but for the first time, I truly felt its claustrophobic weight on the people of Mathare.

Oppression has heft and substance. It clings to those it marks, and it delights in the gravitational pull. If you listen closely, you can hear its voice. *Just give up . . . just give up. It's too much.*

But for all the weight of oppression, there is greater weight in hope. And the hope I've seen in the lives of the women I've met is unlike any hope I've known. It's gritty and tough and can bear the weight of any pain it faces. It's a hope you can go to battle with, a fighting hope that remains even on the darkest days. It reminds me of the water from a garden hose after a long day of digging in dirt. It refreshes and restores even while we are yet on our knees. It requires only that we drink it in.

While we were in Kenya, a new friend named Corazon carefully maneuvered the streets with the team and me. She's a social worker who has walked away from the conveniences of a clinic to embrace splintered benches in a corrugated-metal shanty school. *She's one of them too, one of the women,* I thought to myself as I watched the resolve in her steps and listened to the gentle way she spoke to every person she met, even the ones sitting in the shadows, the ones who were less than welcoming.

"How do you do it, Corazon?" I asked. "How do you not let the weight of the battle crush you here?"

She smiled and said, "I believe the children deserve a chance, but I can do nothing without Jesus Christ. It is all Him."

I thought the weight would be lifted when we traveled to Bungoma County, a place I had been time and time again—a place where Elizabeth would be waiting with a smile and open arms. But the oppression was heavy there too. "Change comes more slowly than we ever desire and with greater speed than we can imagine," Elizabeth said as she stood in her small office that's wallpapered with homemade posters defining rape and outlining how predators captivate their prey. "I believe change is coming. God is here with me."

I think back on the days when answers came easily and solutions were distilled into tidy, alliterative bullet points. The women I've met have taught me that every need met reveals a new and deeper need, every answered prayer is but a new prayer's beginning. Not one believes she is fully qualified—and yet all are fixed on the goal of restoration. They see the depth and magnitude of the battle, and they keep fighting with such grace and resilience.

There's a singular thread that connects the women, the galvanizing force that keeps the gritty, fighting hope alive within them.

The women are resolute. They stay small. They fill the space they are given.

What Real Impact Looks Like

As Miss Mary says, "God does not need you to become big for Him. He wants you to do His work. He will build the stage on which you should stand and give you the people who need to hear what He wants to say."

Like Miss Mary, the women are steadfast, doing their best to keep the main thing the main thing. Small doesn't mean insignificant; rather, it means determined. They aren't swept away by thoughts of notoriety, and they don't allow themselves to be lured by the success of others. And filling space means honoring the time they've been given. The women are all faithful to do good with their hands every day.

I think about Flo, the woman who taught me that there is truly nothing that disqualifies us in this life. She, like Corazon and

Elizabeth, is resolute and focused. She taught me about staying small. You see, if you want to see the difference she's making in the lives of children, you'll have to drive to her home and meet her. She doesn't own a car. The neighborhood she's helped clean up is the one she moved into decades ago. Most of the items she uses to raise funds and care for the people she serves are things others might easily toss in the trash. "People throw away perfectly good things just because they're not fancy enough or not new enough. They'll even throw away brand-new things because they got a fancier new thing," she shared. "But God knows how to take all things and make them beautiful for someone. He's just waiting for us to let Him show us how to use them right."

Staying small for me means tending to those who have been placed in my path. It means more coffee in real life, more conversations with one instead of presentations in front of many, more #kitchentherapy with folks who have names and faces and stories. It means being okay with not being all things to all people at all times.

Flo also taught me about filling the space we are given.

The last time we sat in her living room and talked she said, "I could have moved from this place a long time ago. I've had people promise me all sorts of great things or tell me that I could make something more of myself and never have to worry again about where the money will come from to care for the kids and pay the bills. But this is where I'm most useful."

Rather than filling her time with "if only" wishes, Flo lives her life fully in the midst of her circumstances. "There's a purpose in us being in this place for this time," she said. "If I am going to trust God with my life, that means I trust Him with where my life is right now. And it means I make sure I'm doing the most with this life right now."

Everything around me screams, "Just think of how much *more* you could do if you would just build your platform and leverage your expertise. You could make a *real* impact on this world, you know." But Flo has demonstrated what real impact looks like. The women who have invested in me—the women who are working in remote villages and slums and impoverished neighborhoods, the women who aren't trying to impress folks with their position or power, the women who are relentless in their determination to care for those around them—agree with her. With them as my examples, I am learning to fill the space I'm in.

Be *resolute*.

Stay *small*.

Fill the space you've been given.

I have learned, and I *am* learning, to rest in what I have been taught thus far. But I've got a lot of learning left to do in this life. Did I mention that this is scary? I'm a forgetful soul who isn't always faithful when the days get long. I'm an impatient soul who wants to see results before I've put in the work. I'm a needy soul who likes to be affirmed. I'm a curious soul who comes dangerously close to running off cliffs as I chase illusions.

But Miss Mary and Flo and the other women in this book—they are living out what they are teaching, and that teaching is still transforming me.

They are undaunted, not allowing discouragement to take root. There are hardships, difficult decisions, and seasons when things are simply mundane. But the women see every season as an opportunity to grow, and they find value in the lessons learned.

They keep their hands open. Yes, one of the definitions of *resolute* is "to loosen." And the women who lead give themselves freedom to explore new ideas, ponder new dreams, and invite new ways of thinking and problem solving. They demonstrate that hands are used best when they are open to both give and receive.

Taking the Blows

Even here in my first-world privilege and comfort there is no ignoring the weight of oppression. It puts on different skin and walks with bootstrap confidence, but poverty is as thick in gated communities as it is in garbage dumps. The battle is tidier here, more discreet, tucked away from public view or played out in well-edited vignettes. But it rages, and the whispers of worthlessness never weary. My friends Lisa and Flo see it, feel it, live it. Instead of pondering possibilities, both fix their eyes on Jesus and take the blows for the ones they love.

Hannah dons sequined skirts and stilettos and steps into shadowed streets to rescue young women who find themselves trapped in the grip of sexual exploitation. Her own restored history of abuse, addiction, and self-harm is now writing fresh words of redemption in their stories. She's also become a foster care and adoption counselor, and her home is a welcoming space for children identified by numbers on a file folder. "I'm a mess, but God loves to use messes. That's what I want the kids to know too."

Mirna left a career as an engineer to oversee a government program for girls rescued from abuse and trafficking. "So many nights I have awakened from sleep with a desperate need to pray. I will have the face of one of the girls or the details of one of the rooms on my mind. I believe those prayers have saved lives. Girls who have been raped by their own fathers or have been sold into prostitution by their own mothers—they come with so much pain, and they just want the pain to be gone. I didn't know if I could do this job when I first came—I just knew I needed to be here. I am forever changed now because of the girls. I will stand for them and pray for them. I will fight for them."

Alice and her husband founded two schools in Kenya. She says her culture dictates that the man is the head and the woman is the tail. But she believes the woman is actually the neck that can change culture itself—that God hears the cries of a woman first. "We believe that when you educate a boy, you educate a family, but when you educate a girl, you change a nation. We are here to change nations through the children we're educating. We don't want to leave boys because they are an endangered species in the slum. We want to continue teaching them all and giving them all opportunities. We want to give the girls the morale to know they can do anything, so we always want people to come and talk to them. When they see other people who are good, outstanding in the community, and they are women, they see that they can win over the trauma they are facing in their households. Our women need to see women who are strong."

And there's Susie. She was one of the women who welcomed me to Kenya with songs in 2014, and she and I became sisters when I sat in her humble home and listened to her talk of life as a single mother with HIV. We've shared hugs and tears and prayers over the years. The last time I was in her Kenyan community I heard a familiar name—my own. I turned around and there she was, dressed in a business suit on the back of a boda-boda. "Sister, I am now working!" she exclaimed. "I am helping families in another village, to make them stronger." We celebrated with a dance. And yes, she sang.

I Felt That Your Heart Was Real

This year, I returned to Guatemala and to the sisters who had turned my well-crafted ideas about fixing problems upside down with their bold faith and gumption. It was only fitting that Courtney was with me, and we now watched from the porch as a new team of folks from the United States taught the children about serving each other with integrity. There were far fewer children living in the home now, the result of changes to Guatemalan law and an administration pressed to reintegrate those children into families. Some of the reunions had been successful, but there were also stories of abuse. Only a week before, a terrified young girl had made her way in the dead of night back to the sisters after a family member she had been placed with began beating her. The courts said she could stay.

New kids—children who didn't live at the home but were finding refuge nonetheless—were learning from the team. "They are from a local school," Lourdes said with a slight smile. "They are all struggling in their classes, and their parents are unable to help them because they are illiterate. We heard there were problems, and we thought we could do something."

The sisters then shared a new dream that was growing within them both—a dream reminiscent of their father's heartfelt vision when he sold everything to move to Guatemala. "We believe we can help families outside our gates become stronger so that their children have a better future. We have been given so much here, and we want to share it." Their eyes lit up as they imagined the future, of reading classes and job training and worship on Sundays. "It's good for our children too," Lourdes said. "They are learning to be good neighbors. They are learning to share and to care for others."

Teresa grabbed our hands, and the tears welled in her eyes. "We are not sure how we will do this. But we are given strength because God has answered our prayers before. He is faithful.

"You know, we tell everyone that you are our *angelitas*. When our father passed away in 2008, we were so afraid, we felt so alone. We wanted to honor him, but we did not know how. We prayed for someone to come who would let us know we were loved. We got a call that some Americans wanted to visit. I shook my head. I had such a bad idea of Americans as being cold and cruel. People would come here and take a picture with the children and smile and then never return. But then you came. You asked us what we needed. And you came again to see us. Courtney, when you prayed the first time, I saw you cry, and I felt that your heart was real. You both have become our sisters. You say we have changed the world. This is real. Our world has changed because of you."

The tears fell, and there was no shame.

The women who have taught me to be resolute and to stay small and to fill the space are themselves still learning as they walk against the weight. Their stories are not static moments in time. No, their stories keep unfolding, and that in itself is garden-hose hope to me. Chapters begin and end, joy and heartache hold each other in a tenderly awkward embrace, and dreams are passed like batons to the ones entrusted to keep walking when we no longer can. And we remain resolute.

Yes, I say we, because the women have helped me to see that you and I are *already* women who believe restoration is a reality—even if we don't yet know how to believe. We are uniquely gifted to lead and serve in ways only women can, and our purpose will continue to unfold throughout our journeys. That purpose may not always be something we must find; much more often it will be something discovered like a gemstone within our very circumstances. That purpose is not defined by age or heritage. And no one—including you or me—can disqualify us.

And even as I write these words, I find myself contemplating the story that's unfolding in us. The story that's unfolding in me. I wonder what this story might teach others. And then I hear a familiar voice—the voice of Flo, the modern-day free spirit whose small Austin home is a sanctuary for the vulnerable in her neighborhood. "I get it it now," she told me. "God wants you to write a book to tell these stories, to tell all of His work through common folk like me. I've lived this and I know this. If you do it God's way, it will work."

What I Know about Your Story

Does anyone know where a story begins? I am not sure. But this is what I know about your story—it's what the women have taught me.

No one can disqualify you from your purpose.

You don't have to have all the pieces in place to lead and serve well.

Your purpose will continue to unfold throughout your leadership journey. Don't be afraid.

You are never *not worthy enough* to begin.

Your story can—and will—change. Allow it to do its work.

You are uniquely gifted as a woman to lead creatively. Allow that creativity to rise within you.

Leadership opportunities may be for a season or a lifetime. Both are equal in their power. Embrace the disruptions, and watch God add to your days. You are most beautiful when you bend.

Your purpose will be strengthened by both joy and pain, both success and failure. Embrace it all.

Don't feel that you have to "find your purpose." Often, your calling is hidden like a gemstone in your circumstances.

Don't be afraid to speak up and speak out. Don't be afraid to pray for and pray over. Your purpose has a voice, and God adores it. Speak the language of love.

You are never too old—or too young—to begin.

You can walk in the weight of it all. It's time to drink the water from the garden hose of gritty fighting hope. You can be resolute, stay small, and fill the space you've been given. One woman can change the world, and God says, "That woman is you."

Postscript

You've just read a book about a God whose purpose for you is expansive and encompassing. Ephesians 2:10 tells us ways He has etched heaven's poetry on our lives to accomplish magnificent things, and Ephesians 3:20 says His creativity within us is greater than anything we could imagine. His story within us is filled with plot twists and mystery and comedy and suspense—and it's deeper and higher and wider than any page could hold.

He's got you. He calls you beloved. He delights in you.

I'll close with a blessing for the women—and for you—as they reclaim God's powerful design:

Oh, faithful ones, my precious loves, may grace find you and cover you in its presence, may grace sustain you and warm you and comfort you. My heart has longed for you to be comforted since the first day I met you. You labor hard and long for love to be lavished on all you meet; your backs are bowed from years of stooping low to lift others high. The gospel is not simply a biography you recite to others; it is the lifeblood of a living Jesus flowing through you to the lowest and the least. It is healing, it is heartbeat, it is hope upon hope upon hope. You are a well, pouring out vibrant, effervescent life, its joy splashing on your faces. Your faces are radiant.

And so I pray now for you, for your souls to be filled to overflowing with the words of our Lord's will, for your mouths to be filled with His Good News message, for your backs to be strengthened to keep carrying the load. I pray for you to walk tall and run strong and dance joyfully. You are the image of who I long to be—and who the Lord is making me to be. I give the greatest thanks to our Father for you, for He has made you beautiful.

Acknowledgments

As best as I can tell, it was 2015 when I started ending blog posts and love notes with "We're in this together." It started with a story titled "Remembering What's Good," a story filled with beautiful and purposeful things.

If I were to write that story right now, it would most certainly include the following people. We're in this together, and I am better for it.

To Jesus: You remain the life in my veins.

To the women in this book: You truly have changed the way I see life, death, love, justice, women, men, faith, grace, hope, and even myself. This writer is ill-equipped to find the words to thank you adequately. I can't wait for the world to get to know you and for some folks to even meet you in person.

To the women in the Scriptures: Gosh, how powerful your stories become when I see them through the lens of God's design for us. I've fallen in love with you over and over again.

To my agent, Karen, at Credo: You saw this book in its fullness when I saw only pieces. Thank you for the warm welcome, the gut-level honesty, the sage wisdom, and the passion you have for fine detail. My next tattoo just might be an em dash.

To Kelsey at Revell: Thank you for the Tuesday afternoon kindness when you first said, "I want to read this book." Thank you for every comment in the margins and for reminding me that words edited are words that can still find a home. To Robin: My ever-present calming force in the midst of the shape-shifting and refining of the manuscript, bless you. Would you both please hug the rest of the Revell team for me? They've done well. We've done well.

To Elora: You remain my Charlotte, the weaver of the words I need to remember about who I am. Thank you for the persistent grace.

To Ann and Mary: Thank you for saying "I'll listen!" when I needed more than tutorials to let me know I was on the right path. And to Renee: Thank you for sparking bravery in me to stay the course.

To Dana, Kaylei, Julia, and Teri: This book wouldn't have come to life without you. Honestly. I'm in tears now.

To Amanda: Thank you for encouraging me to submit the proposal. One day I will read *your* books, and they will be glorious. Until then, keep reminding everyone of the power of words and the beauty of a Chicago metro ride in the morning.

And to the literary agent who told me years ago there wasn't a place on a bookshelf for words like mine: Thank you. When someone tells this renegade free spirit no, it inspires me to find the yes.

To my GGGs: I would travel the world with you to gather hope over and over again.

To Middy: How grateful I am to keep walking this winding road with you.

To Alison: I'll meet you in every tomorrow. Felix culpa.

To Melissa: My #blueandbraided, I am thankful for Twitter profiles that weave lives together in a most beautiful way.

To Kate, KJ, Tracy, Rebecca, Nate, Jolene, and Traci: You cheered, encouraged, challenged, and offered a safe place for this writer's wonderings to land. Thank you. Thank you, too, to Hope*Writers, Redbud Writers Guild, Rise Up Writers, and the original sisters of the Story Sessions. I have learned so much from all of you, and I am still learning. And in the midst of all the chaos and noise, there are voices that always calm my soul. Amy, Andrea, Ronei, Cathy, Sarah, Tammy, and Heather are those voices to me.

To Aaron, Matt, Rick, D$, David, Derek, Tivo, and Rohit: I'd be lost without the wraparound kindness of you. You nudge me every time I say that my writing is just for women, reminding me that divine words have power beyond boundaries.

To Jon, the community of Dreamers and Builders, and the Launch Out gang: Thank you for listening to me speak. Thank you for saying my words meant something. Jon, give Jenny a hug for me. She should be in this book.

To Mike, Tiffany, the Amys, and my worldwide family at Orphan Outreach: I am humbled to serve alongside you, honored to tell stories that change stories because of your selfless work, and I'm grateful for your transparency and accountability in doing what's in the best interest of each and every orphaned and vulnerable child. When it comes to honoring women in leadership, you are most worthy role models. Every chapter in this book has your fingerprints on it in some way. What a joy it is to be able to donate a portion of the proceeds of the sale of this book to the good work being done around the globe. There are so many more stories to share.

To Courtney and Niki: Thank you for Sunday nights at the table, for the deeper conversations that always happen in the kitchen, and for the warrior prayers all the days in between. Court, new adventures await.

To Brad, Ian, and Gina: Your love steadies me. Thank you for putting up with all my ebbs and flows.

To Sawyer: We will always be words people. Thank you for asking what I'm writing and for listening to what's on the page. You will always make my heart melt (Poppa and Daddy don't mind at all).

And to Tyler: One day I'll write a book about you, because you, my love, will change the world too.

Notes

Chapter 2 Let's Talk about You

1. Carolyn Curtis James, "The Ezer-Kenegdo: Ezer Unleashed," *Faith Gateway* (blog), March 20, 2015, https://www.faithgateway.com/ezer-unleashed/#.Xfgd3NZKgWo.

2. Jordan Gaines Lewis, "When It Comes to Color, Men and Women Aren't Seeing Eye to Eye," Psychology Today, April 8, 2015, https://www.psychologytoday.com/us/blog/brain-babble/201504/when-it-comes-color-men-women-arent-seeing-eye-eye?amp.

3. "Why Did the Edge Walk Off the Edge? The Answer Might Surprise You," Inside the Brain, May 16, 2015, https://inside-the-brain.com/tag/peripheral-vision/.

4. Hanan Parvez, "Are Women Better Listeners Than Men," PsychMechanics, July 5, 2017, https://www.psychmechanics.com/2017/07/how-men-and-women-hear-things.html.

5. Bruce Goldman, "Two Minds: The Cognitive Differences between Men and Women," *Stanford Medicine*, Spring 2017, https://stanmed.stanford.edu/2017spring/how-mens-and-womens-brains-are-different.html.

6. Bob Grant, "Male and Female Brains Wired Differently," *Scientist*, December 4, 2013, https://www.the-scientist.com/the-nutshell/male-and-female-brains-wired-differently-38304.

7. Goldman, "Two Minds."

Chapter 7 God's Purpose Is *You*

1. Emily P. Freeman, "Create a Simple Morning Routine," *The Next Right Thing* (podcast), March 26, 2019, https://emilypfreeman.com/podcast/the-next-right-thing/76/. Her book *The Next Right Thing* is also available.

Chapter 13 Tia Lilly and Lucy

1. To read the beautiful words of Daniel Whittle's hymn, "Not My Own, But Saved by Jesus," please visit https://hymnary.org/text/not_my_own_but_saved_by_jesus.

Chapter 21 What Others Need to Hear

1. "In Between the Man and the Message," YouTube video, from an interview with Eugene Peterson, posted by "NavPress," August 30, 2016, https://www.you tube.com/watch?v=LaMgIvbXqSk.

Chapter 22 Lisa and Bianca

1. Charles Colson, *Being the Body: A New Call for the Church to be Light in the Darkness* (Nashville: Thomas Nelson, 2003), chap. 27, Kindle.
2. Colson, *Being the Body*, loc. 7183 of 9968, Kindle.

Chapter 26 Take Courage

1. "A History of Veronica 01: The Woman," *Sacrificium Laudis* (blog), December 12, 2013, http://sacrificium-laudis.blogspot.com/2013/12/a-history-of -veronica-part-01-woman.html.

Ronne Rock weaves themes of transformative hope and grace-filled leadership into everything she shares on page and stage. An award-winning marketing and communications executive in both the corporate and nonprofit sectors, she now shares her more than thirty years of expertise in creative leadership with faith-based organizations. Ronne also travels around the world to gather words and images that inspire others to action with Orphan Outreach, a global nonprofit dedicated to serving the orphaned and vulnerable. She's a writer, blogger, and speaker—sharing battle-tested wisdom about leadership, advocacy marketing, and finding God in the most beautiful and painful of circumstances. An Oklahoma gal by birth, Ronne now lives in Austin, Texas, with her husband, Brad, and rescue pup, Pearl. Her son and his family live in Arizona, which Ronne has deemed way too far away.

CONNECT WITH *Ronne*

RONNEROCK.COM

 RonneRockWrites

 RonneRock

LET'S RESTORE HOPE
together.

The orphan crisis is complex but serving orphaned and vulnerable children doesn't have to be complicated. We have five ways you can make a difference today. **Visit OrphanOutreach.org/MakeADifference.**

Proceeds from the purchase of this book support the ministry programs of Orphan Outreach.

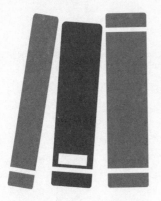

LIKE THIS BOOK?

Consider sharing it with others!

- Share or mention the book on your social media platforms. Use the hashtag **#OneWomanCanChangeTheWorld**.

- Write a book review on your blog or on a retailer site.

- Pick up a copy for friends, family, or anyone who you think would enjoy and be challenged by its message!

- Share this message on Twitter, Facebook, or Instagram: **I loved #OneWomanCanChangeTheWorld by @RonneRock @ReadBakerBooks**

- Recommend this book for your church, workplace, book club, or class.

- Follow Baker Books on social media and tell us what you like.

ReadBakerBooks

ReadBakerBooks

ReadBakerBooks